Artificial Intelligence

An Executive Guide to Make AI Work for Your Business

David E. Sweenor

It's not the tech that's tiny, just the book!™

TinyTechMedia LLC

Artificial Intelligence: An Executive Guide to Make AI Work for Your Business

by David E. Sweenor

Published By:

TinyTechMedia LLC

Editor: Taylor Porter

Cover Designer: Josipa Caran Safradin

Proofreader / Indexer: Peter Letzelter-Smith

Typesetter / Layout: Daria Lacy

April 2022: First Edition

Revision History for the First Edition

2022-04-02: First Release

ISBN: 979-8-9858227-0-0 (paperback)

ISBN: 979-8-9858227-1-7 (eBook)

In Praise Of

There are many books out there explaining artificial intelligence in great detail. Most people will not have the time or interest to read those books. I read the TinyTechGuide Artificial Intelligence: An Executive Guide to Make AI Work for Your Business in just under two hours. The book is informative, useful, and practical. If you are a business manager or executive who needs to understand the foundational elements of AI and how it is being used, this book is for you.

John K. Thompson, 2X best-selling author, analytics innovator, and keynote speaker/ thought leader on data and analytics

The industry is rife with confusion surrounding AI, data science, and machine learning. Thankfully, David's guide provides a well-written and accessible guide for business managers to better understand their nuances and be equipped to knowledgeably participate in related business discussions.

Howard Dresner, founder and chief research officer, Dresner Advisory Services

TinyTechGuide's intro to artificial intelligence is an excellent primer to help demystify the best practices of automating with analytics. With the essentials of terminology, overviews of popular techniques, as well as sharing powerful frameworks for managing AI in the real world, this guide will help chart a course for your own journey into making smarter decisions with your data!

Nick Jewell, PhD, co-founder of *datacurious.ai*

The Artificial Intelligence: An Executive Guide to Make AI Work for Your Business provides a great overview of the applications of AI across various industries. It's perfect for individuals that simply do not have enough time in the day to learn about the latest technology trends. I especially loved the examples of AI in action!

Kate Strachnyi, founder of DATAcated

It is imperative that business leaders understand how they can put AI to work to support their company's revenue growth. Without a clear understanding of AI, business leaders may make poor choices. David Sweenor provides a critical resource that is highly accessible.

Judith Hurwitz, thought leader and consultant in causal AI

Sweenor's book on AI is both well targeted and well timed. In order to succeed with AI, organizations need their business people to understand and apply the technology. And AI is increasingly becoming usable by "citizen data scientists" with only basic quantitative skills. This is a great source if you want to actively participate in the AI revolution that is sweeping business.

Thomas H. Davenport, distinguished professor at Babson College and visiting professor at Oxford Saïd Business School, author of The AI Advantage and Competing on Analytics

An excellent comprehensive guide to deep dive into AI infrastructure. David made it super easy for even non-technical professionals to understand artificial intelligence in depth. The guide explains the relationship between data, analytics, and automation. It's simple: If you are not leveraging AI and machine learning for real decision-making, you might feel disrupted by competitors in the future. Highly recommend this guide to understand the AI revolution.

Ravit Jain, founder and host of The Ravit Show, Data Evangelist

Executives that understand AI are the most valuable and rare resource on the planet, and David Sweenor's TinyTechGuide is the fastest way for leaders to become AI literate. Even more importantly, it teaches you the fundamentals of how to drive business outcomes with AI.

Kjell Carlsson, PhD, AI strategist and evangelist, former Forrester analyst

A well set out bite sized deep dive into AI. From defining what AI really is, through insights on the people, tech and processes, to ethical considerations this TinyTechGuide packs a thought provoking punch. As the title suggests this really is a guide to make AI work for your business.

Al Herron, head of product marketing

Dedication

To my wonderful wife, Erin, for her unwavering support and unconditional love. Without her, I would be lost and TinyTechGuides would not exist.

To my son Andy, for his focus, honesty, and determination.

To my son Chris, for his creativity, enthusiasm, and humor.

To my parents, Rita and David. Without them, none of this would have been possible.

Contents

Chapter 3

Chapter 5

Chapter 6

Chapter 7

Chapter 8

Prologue

TinyTechGuides are designed for practitioners, business leaders, and executives who never seem to have enough time to learn about the latest technology trends. These guides are designed to be read in an hour or two and focus on the application of technologies in a business, government, or educational institution.

After reading this guide, it's my hope that you'll have a better understanding of the technology and a better idea of how to apply it in your business or organization.

Wherever possible, I try to share best practices and lessons learned over my career so you can take this learning and transform it into action.

Remember, it's not the tech that's tiny, just the book!™

If you're interested in writing a TinyTechGuide, please visit TinyTechGuides.com.

Chapter 1

Introduction

Who Is This Book For?

For some, the term artificial intelligence (AI) reminds them of Skynet and *The Terminator*. For others, it conjures ideas of a better society with self-driving cars, food security, medical breakthroughs, and unbounded potential to help people. For many business leaders, the very term "AI" is vague, confusing, and—although intriguing— seemingly just out of reach. With advancements in AI being used to accelerate innovation and productivity, reduce costs and risks, and improve overall business results, it's important for all business leaders to have a clear understanding of what artificial intelligence is and how it can be applied to their businesses.

If you're an expert in data science, machine learning, artificial intelligence, or automation technologies, this book is not for you. It is designed for business teams, managers, business leaders, and executives to provide a clear and non-technical assessment of how people are using artificial intelligence across different lines of business and industries.

After reading this book, you'll have a better understanding of:

- What AI is and how it's applied across different business use cases
- The difference between artificial intelligence and machine learning
- A high-level overview of how AI works
- Practical advice on how to start using AI

How Is This Book Organized?

This book is organized into eight chapters. The first explains the basics of AI, where it's used, and how it can improve business results. The following chapters provide a deeper look at each of the core topics mentioned in Chapter 1. Chapter 2 dives into what AI boils down to. Chapter 3 discusses how AI works and the core technologies behind it. Chapter 4 covers AI usage across departments and industries. Chapter 5 examines different types of business decisions and the benefits of AI. Chapter 6 shows you how to get started, while Chapter 7 looks at the ethical considerations of AI. Lastly, Chapter 8 provides a framework for you to consider on your AI journey. I have tried to include as many different use cases as possible to help you gain a better understanding of how AI is implemented across industries and business functions—and to help you do the same.

What Is Artificial Intelligence?

Broadly speaking, when people hear the term artificial intelligence (AI), they generally attribute it to machines being able to think and act like humans. In other words, they think AI can interpret the world and make human-like decisions. This is too vague.

Digging a little deeper, AI is often segmented into two categories:

- **Artificial General Intelligence** (AGI), also referred to as "strong AI" or "general AI"
- **Artificial Narrow Intelligence** (ANI), also referred to as "narrow AI"

Simply stated, Artificial General Intelligence is the realm of science fiction. Depending on your preference, AGI may be HAL from Stanley Kubrick's *2001: A Space Odyssey*, Arnold Schwarzenegger in *The Terminator*, or Ava from *Ex Machina*. In these movies, the villains exhibit human-like traits and abilities that would certainly pass the Turing Test.

 A computer would deserve to be called intelligent if it could deceive a human into believing that it was human."[1]

—Alan Turing

Of course, passing the Turing Test isn't a requirement of AGI. Remember "Eugene Goostman" in 2014? Posing as a 13-year-old Ukrainian boy, this smart chatbot was able to convince 33% of the judges at the Royal Society of London that it was human.[2]

Unlike AGI, Artificial Narrow Intelligence is the technology of today. Executives are using its power across all lines of business and industries. ANI is simply data, analytics, and automation technology used to solve very specific tasks.

That's it. No robotic apocalypse. No sentient machines. Just data, analytics, and automation.

Examples include:

- Using **chatbots and conversational AI** to accomplish specific tasks like opening a bank account or ordering a pizza. (This improves the quality of customer service and lowers operating costs.)

- Using **predictive analytics and machine learning** algorithms to hyper-personalize offers and customer experiences in real-time. (This leads to higher revenue, lower costs, and improved customer satisfaction.)

- Using **computer vision and optical character recognition** (OCR) to extract text data from receipts, invoices, and PDF files to automate warranty claims or sift through siloed data sources to select the right candidates for pharmaceutical clinical trials. (This can lower costs, improve satisfaction, and reduce risks.)

- Using **natural language processing (NLP) and text analytics** to identify key themes and sentiment in text data. Better understanding the voice of the customer leads to improving service quality and recommending next-best actions. (This can increase revenue, reduce manual intervention, and improve efficiency.)

- Applying **computer vision** to automatically scan images and identify anomalies in medical images or manufacturing defects. (This can improve diagnosis, reduce costs, and improve quality.)

Unless explicitly stated, we will simply use the term AI to refer to Artificial Narrow Intelligence, the stuff of modern AI—the technology of today.

How Does AI Work?

To make AI work, one needs to combine different types of technology that already exist in many enterprises. First and foremost, it begins with the raw ingredient: data. This is the foundation of AI and comes in all shapes and sizes. Data, essentially, represents a set of facts, which can be numbers, text, documents, video, images, log files, geospatial information, or audio.

Let's assume that the data is clean, of sufficient quality, and unbiased. At the highest level, to make AI work, one needs to combine this data with analytics and digital automation technology to solve a specific task or business problem.

Artificial Intelligence = Data + Analytics + Automation

Analytics can take many forms, but there are generally four broad categories: descriptive, diagnostic, predictive, and prescriptive. I'll describe these in a bit more detail in Chapter 2. Organizations can, and often do, apply these analytic techniques to derive insights from data, but on its own this is not enough. An example of an insight could be that we expect a 20% increase in COVID-19 hospitalizations next month. This is a great insight, but as a healthcare provider, what should I do with this? Should I order more supplies to prevent a stockout, increase staffing levels, or increase the hospital's capacity by adding more beds? The analytic insights need to be applied to specific business problems to make decisions that, in turn, cause the business to take beneficial action.

If the business does not take action or change its behavior as a result of the AI-based decision, why bother?

Figure 1.1 illustrates the data to insights to action framework.

Figure 1.1: Data to Insight to Action Framework

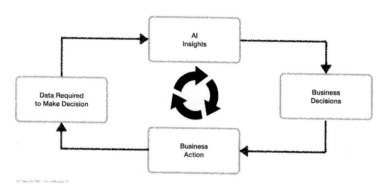

Now, in order to transform this into AI, we need to apply digital automation technologies. By fusing analytics and automation technology together, a business has successfully implemented AI. Of course, these systems can become quite complex and need to be monitored and governed, but nevertheless, the concept is simple. Figure 1.2 provides a pragmatic definition of AI.

Figure 1.2: A Practical Definition of AI

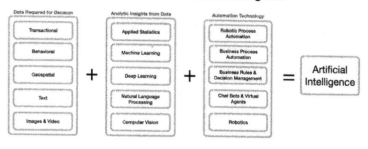

There are many terms used interchangeably to describe AI. Analytics terminology includes predictive analytics, machine learning, neural networks, deep learning, natural language processing (NLP), natural language generation (NLG), computer vision, chatbots, optimization, and many others. Simply put: *It's All Analytics!*[8]

Many consider machine learning (ML) as one of the foundational technologies used for AI. I discuss the relationship between AI and ML in Chapter 2 and specific ML techniques in Chapter 3. In many cases, ML is used to create predictive models that can make educated guesses on what's likely to happen in the future. Pretty useful, right? Fundamentally, predictive models are mathematical formulas created by "learning" the patterns contained in historical data. These algorithms are then applied to new data to make a prediction, which is simply a probability that something is likely to happen and often with very high accuracy.

Automation technologies include methods that run from the simple scheduling of workflows or pipelines to things like chatbots, virtual agents, robotic process automation (RPA), business process automation (BPA), analytics automation, and others. By fusing these two technologies together—and designing them to solve a specific task, make a decision, or solve a specific problem—one is applying artificial intelligence.

Where Is AI Being Used?

Now that we have a pragmatic definition of AI, let's look at how it is being applied across departments and industries. I'll cover this more extensively in Chapter 4. Although this is by no means a comprehensive list of departments, industries, or use cases, it's my hope that the information below can provide a solid foundation for understanding how organizations apply AI to solve specific business problems.

AI Use By Department

Figure 1.3 illustrates common use cases for artificial intelligence.

Figure 1.3: AI Use Cases By Department

Some examples of businesses using AI:

- **Dominos**, the largest pizza company in the world, uses chatbots that allow customers to order pizzas from Google Home, Amazon Alexa, or a Smart TV.[4] It also uses computer vision to improve the pizza quality and the distribution of toppings while piloting pizza delivery with self-driving vehicles.[5,6]

- **John Deere**, an agricultural equipment manufacturer, uses AI to improve welding quality on its machines.[7] It has also developed an autonomous self-driving tractor that can plow, sow seeds, and even avoid obstacles.[8] It provides an app to farmers with live video, image, metrics, and options to change the tractor's speed.[9]

- **JPMorgan Chase**, the banking behemoth, uses AI to help tag and classify documents that customers uploaded as part of the US federal government's Paycheck Protection Program (PPP) that was enacted in response to COVID-19. It also uses it to personalize marketing messages and detect fraud, which has been successfully decreased by over \$100M per year.[10] AI is also used for anomaly detection, text extraction from documents, and pricing optimization.[11]

AI Use By Industry

AI is now used across every industry. However, some are more mature using it.

Figure 1.4 shows the most mature industries that have adopted AI. Retail leads the pack, followed by Financial Services and Telecommunications, while Education continues to lag.[12]

Figure 1.4: AI Adoption By Industry

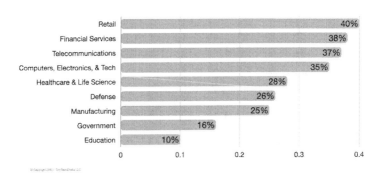

The key AI technologies being used are analytics technologies—like computer vision, machine learning, and natural language processing—and automation technologies like virtual agents, chatbots, physical robotics, and autonomous vehicles.

Why Are Companies Adopting AI?

If the COVID-19 pandemic has taught us anything, it's that organizations need to be adaptable. Multi-year plans were put into high gear. In fact, **Frito-Lay** reported accelerating digital initiatives that were expected to take five years to about six months.[13] Smart companies are making AI a core tenant of their business and digital strategy. By applying AI and technology to businesses, organizations are seeing cost reductions and revenue and efficiency gains.

Based on a survey conducted by McKinsey, business leaders were asked to rate the relative cost reductions or revenue increases that resulted from implementing AI.[14]

Figure 1.5 illustrates some of these, categorized into cost reductions of less than 10%, between 10% and 19%, and greater than 20%. From the graph, you can see that 51% of survey respondents indicated that Sales Operations had cost reductions in excess of 20% compared to an average of 33% across all functions. Figure 1.6 highlights revenue increases due to AI adoption.

Figure 1.5 Cost Reductions from AI Adoption

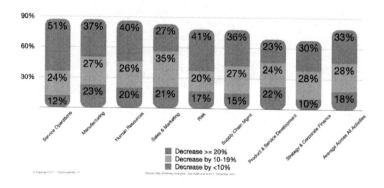

Figure 1.6: Revenue Increases from AI Initiatives

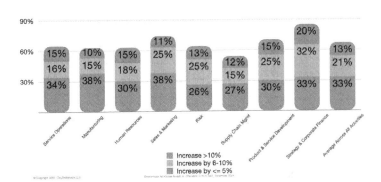

AI can create significant value for organizations.[15] Aside from revenue, the top reasons to adopt AI include:

- **Reduced costs**: Eliminate unnecessary human-hours by automating routine, repetitive, and mundane tasks. Examples include using natural language processing to open accounts and schedule appointments.

- **Faster execution**: Accelerate time-to-value and automate responses. Examples include drug approvals.

- **Reduced complexity**: Aggregate data across complex sources to simplify and streamline decision-making with predictive and prescriptive analytics. Examples include predictive maintenance and supply chain optimization.

- **Hyper-personalized experiences**: Transform customer engagement using machine learning, sentiment analytics, and predictive analytics to improve customer engagement.

- **Accelerated innovation**: Create new products, services, and business models based on customer needs, usage patterns, sentiment, and behaviors.

11

- **Improved trust**: Improve consistency and accountability to boost trust with customers. AI can be used to proactively identify fraud, expand cybersecurity, and prevent privacy breaches before they occur.

Getting Started With AI

To increase your chances of success with AI, use these best practices that have been implemented by top-performing companies:[16]

- Align AI strategy and business goals
- Upskill employees for AI
- Collaborate cross-functionally
- Implement data governance
- Standardize and automate business practices
- Ensure adoption and value

In Chapter 5, I'll dig into the specific quantitative benefits of specific practices.

But before that, here's a quick self-assessment to see where your organization stands with regards to AI maturity:

1. Does your organization have an AI strategy with a roadmap of use cases?

2. Is your AI strategy aligned with the business strategy?

3. Do you have AI learning programs in place for employees?

4. Do you have cross-functional teams formed to deliver AI projects?

5. Do you have a data strategy that supports AI?

6. Do you have a data governance strategy in place?

7. Do you have AI tools in place for your business teams to use?

8. Do you have a process in place to monitor and update AI models?

9. Have you employed design thinking to ensure frontline employees use AI in their daily decision-making?

10. Do you regularly monitor and track AI projects against well-defined key performance indicators (KPIs)?

So, how did you do? What was your grade? Did you answer "yes" to at least six of these? Is a 60% grade good enough for your organization to remain competitive? Ideally, your company would reach 90% or 100%.

Ethical Considerations

Unlike typical enterprise software, organizations need to pay particular attention to both data and AI ethics, also known as responsible AI. Because of its broad ranging applicability and the power to adversely impact lives, AI must be closely monitored. There are no shortages of stories about AI going awry and causing harm to individuals and populations.

Examples include:

- *The New York Times* reported that the **Apple credit card** granted levels of credit 20 times higher to a husband compared to a wife who filled out the same application.[17] However, after an investigation, it turned out that it wasn't biased against women, but the reputational damage had already been done.

- Widespread racial bias in facial recognition algorithms, which have the worst accuracy with dark-skinned females.[18]

- **Amazon's** hiring algorithm was biased against women because the training data used for it had more men.[19]

- Black defendants in criminal trials were twice as likely to be misclassified as a higher risk for re-offending (aka recidivism) by the **COMPAS** (Correctional Offender Management Profiling for Alternative Sanctions) algorithm.[20]

- A news article about researchers studying a biased healthcare algorithm from **Optum Health** stated: "black patients assigned the same level of risk by the algorithm are actually sicker than white patients, but bias occurs because the algorithm uses health costs as the measure for health needs."[21]

To help provide a framework for how companies should think about AI ethics, I provide an overview in Figure 1.6. I'll explore this topic more in Chapter 7.

Figure 1.6: AI Ethics Framework

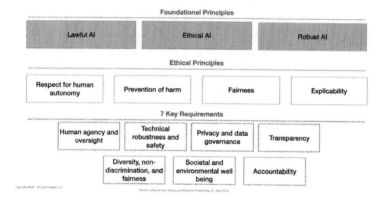

Summary

In this chapter, we learned what comprises AI. We saw how **data + analytics + automation** is used across different companies and use cases. We then looked at how top-performing companies use AI and concluded with ethical considerations. The remainder of this book will go through each of these topics in more detail.

Chapter 1 References

1   Cooper, S. Barry. "Alan Turing: 'I Am Building a Brain';
    Half a Century Later, Its Successor Beat Kasparov."
    Guardian. May 14, 2012. https://www.theguardian.com/uk/
    the-northerner/2012/may/14/alan-turing-gary-kasparov-
    computer.

2   Schofield, Jack. "Computer Chatbot 'Eugene Goostman'
    Passes the Turing Test." ZDNet. June 8, 2014. https://www.
    zdnet.com/article/computer-chatbot-eugene-goostman-
    passes-the-turing-test/.

3   Burk, Scott, David Sweenor, and Gary Miner. It's All
    Analytics—Part II: Designing an Integrated Ai, Analytics, and
    Data Science … Architecture for Your Organization. Boca
    Raton, FL: CRC Press, 2021.

4   "Domino's Anyware." Domino's Anyware. 2013. https://
    anyware.dominos.com/.

5   "DOM Pizza Checker." DOM Pizza Checker. 2019. https://
    dompizzachecker.dominos.com.au/.

6   Etherington, Darrell. "Domino's Serves up Self-Driving
    Pizza Delivery Pilot in Houston." TechCrunch. June 17, 2019.
    https://techcrunch.com/2019/06/17/
    dominos-serves-up-self-driving-pizza-delivery-pilot-in-
    houston/.

7   "At John Deere, 'Hard Iron Meets Artificial Intelligence.'"
    InsideBIGDATA. April 5, 2021. https://insidebigdata.
    com/2021/04/05/at-john-deere-hard-iron-meets-artificial-
    intelligence/.

8   Knight, Will. "John Deere's Self-Driving Tractor Stirs Debate
    on AI in Farming." Wired. January 4, 2022. https://www.wired.
    com/story/john-deere-self-driving-tractor-stirs-debate-ai-
    farming/.

9   "John Deere Reveals Fully Autonomous Tractor at CES 2022." Deere.com. January 4, 2022. https://www.deere.com/en/news/all-news/autonomous-tractor-reveal/.

10 Sawers, Paul. "How Chase Is Using AI to Update Banking." VentureBeat. July 15, 2020. https://venturebeat.com/2020/07/15/how-chase-is-using-ai-to-update-banking/.

11 SR2020. "Robo-Banking: Artificial Intelligence at JPMorgan Chase." Digital Innovation and Transformation. April 21, 2020. https://digital.hbs.edu/platform-digit/submission/robo-banking-artificial-intelligence-at-jpmorgan-chase/.

12 Cam, Arif, Michael Chui, and Bryce Hall. "Survey: AI Adoption Proves Its Worth, but Few Scale Impact | McKinsey." McKinsey. September 2019. https://www.mckinsey.com/featured-insights/artificial-intelligence/global-ai-survey-ai-proves-its-worth-but-few-scale-impact.

13 McKendrick, Joe. "AI Adoption Skyrocketed over the Last 18 Months." Harvard Business Review, September 27, 2021. https://hbr.org/2021/09/ai-adoption-skyrocketed-over-the-last-18-months.

14 "Global AI Survey: AI Proves Its Worth, but Few Scale Impact." McKinsey. November 22, 2019. https://www.mckinsey.com/featured-insights/artificial-intelligence/global-ai-survey-ai-proves-its-worth-but-few-scale-impact.

15 "Industry Applications of AI." Deloitte United States. n.d. Accessed January 17, 2022. https://www2.deloitte.com/us/en/pages/consulting/articles/ai-dossier.html.

16 "Survey: AI Adoption Proves Its Worth, but Few Scale Impact." McKinsey. November 22, 2019. https://www.mckinsey.com/featured-insights/artificial-intelligence/global-ai-survey-ai-proves-its-worth-but-few-scale-impact.

17 Smith, Genevieve, and Ishita Rustagi. "When Good Algorithms Go Sexist: Why and How to Advance AI Gender Equity." Stanford Social Innovation Review. March 31, 2021. https://ssir.org/articles/entry/

when_good_algorithms_go_sexist_why_and_how_to_
advance_ai_gender_equity.

18   Najibi, Alex. "Racial Discrimination in Face Recognition
Technology." Science In The News. October 24, 2020. https://
sitn.hms.harvard.edu/flash/2020/racial-discrimination-in-face-
recognition-technology/.

19   Dastin, Jeffrey. "Amazon Scraps Secret AI Recruiting Tool
That Showed Bias against Women." Reuters. October 10,
2018. https://www.reuters.com/article/us-amazon-com-jobs-
automation-insight/amazon-scraps-secret-ai-recruiting-tool-
that-showed-bias-against-women-idUSKCN1MK08G.

20   Larson, Jeff, Surya Mattu, Lauren Kirchner, and Julia
Angwin. "How We Analyzed the COMPAS Recidivism
Algorithm." ProPublica. May 23, 2016. https://www.
propublica.org/article/how-we-analyzed-the-compas-
recidivism-algorithm.

21   Morse, Susan. "Study Finds Racial Bias in Optum
Algorithms." Healthcare Finance News. October 25, 2019.
https://www.healthcarefinancenews.com/
news/study-finds-racial-bias-optum-algorithm.

Chapter 2

What Is Artificial Intelligence?

As mentioned in Chapter 1, people have quite varied definitions of artificial intelligence (AI). Whether they have Rosie the Robot from *The Jetsons* on their mind or a character from the HBO series *Westworld*, interpretations are often far from reality. The fact of the matter is that AI is a bit more approachable than most people think. Along with data and automation technologies, analytics is a foundational pillar to create AI. Let's examine different analytic techniques in the next section.

Analytics 101

Before we delve directly into AI, we need to make sure we are aligned with our terminology. Analytics is generally categorized into four broad categories: descriptive, diagnostic, predictive, and prescriptive. Table 2.1 summarizes the different types of analytics, showing the business questions to be answered, the best type of analytics to use, and example use cases. Most organizations use a combination of analytic types to gain a competitive advantage.

Table 2.1: Business Questions, Use Cases, and Analytic Types

Business Question	Analytic Type	Example Use Case
What happened?	Descriptive	• What were last week's sales?
Why did it happen?	Diagnostic	• What caused our sales to increase last week? • What were the top 10 defects that caused our car yield to decrease last month? • What are the primary reasons the insurance claims are being filed?
What is likely to happen?	Predictive	• Given past trends, what is the next quarter's sales forecast? • When is the equipment in our factory going to break down? • Given current conditions, how long do we expect elevated insurance claims to persist?

What should we do?	Prescriptive	• Given our sales projections, we recommend running incentives to our sales teams to encourage selling a specific bundle.
		• Given the likelihood of equipment failure, we recommend performing maintenance next week.
		• To reduce customer churn, please offer customers the promotion code PROMO20 to stay with our company.

Descriptive Analytics: What Happened?

Descriptive analytics is the most common type used in organizations—and in life. Take a look at today's newspaper—there's a good chance you'll see descriptive analytics in action. These may be summary tables, graphs, pie charts, trend charts, and the like. They're used to summarize data and answer the question: "**What happened?**" An example is this table summarizing medal counts at the Beijing Olympics, as illustrated in Figure 2.1.

Figure 2.1: Medal Counts at Beijing Olympics

Beijing Winter Olympic Medal Counts

Country	Gold	Silver	Bronze	Total
Norway	16	8	13	37
Germany	12	10	5	27
China	9	4	2	27
United States	8	10	7	25
Sweden	8	5	5	18

Another example of descriptive analytics is from the US Centers for Disease Control and Prevention in Figure 2.2.

As you can see, descriptive analytics are quite common and familiar.

Figure 2.2: COVID-19 Trends in the United States

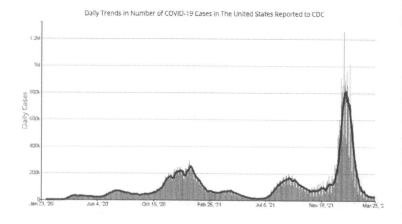

Diagnostic Analytics: Why Did It Happen?

Now that we understand what descriptive analytics is, let's move to diagnostic analytics, which is designed to answer the question "**Why did it happen?**" Diagnostic analytics are also very common. To understand them in action, let's look at the US economy. As of the writing of this book, inflation is the highest it has been in four decades at 7.5%! So, the 7.5% is the descriptive analytic. Diagnostic analytics answers the **why**. What causes inflation? Inflation occurs either due to an increase in prices of goods and services or a fall in the value of money. For the current record inflation levels in the United States, inflation is at its highest due to a variety of factors:

- Increased savings from government stimulus programs
- Lower spending on services due to business restrictions
- Fewer workers in the labor market
- Low interest rates
- Increased energy prices
- Supply chain disruptions
- Semiconductor shortages

These factors are diagnostic analytics in action. We could go further and attempt to quantify how much each of these contributes to inflation but that is beyond the scope of this example.

Predictive Analytics: What Is Likely to Happen?

Now that we have a better understanding of the different types of business questions that analytics can answer, let's turn our focus to predictive and prescriptive analytics—the foundation of technology used for AI. The most common method employed in AI is machine learning (ML) technology. With ML, analysts and data scientists will often refer to models and then deploying models into business systems. A model is nothing more than a mathematical formula or algorithm.

Remember the formula "y=mx + b" from basic algebra? This is an equation or model for a straight line where m is the slope of the line and b is the y-intercept (where it crosses the y-axis). Now, we need not go into details about how to draw the best fit line through a set of points on a 2D (x/y) graph, but it involves minimizing some sort of error function. All you really need to know is that there are known methods for how to perform these computations. And these days, after you formulate the problem and prepare your data, the computer does most of the work!

Now, there are many different types of algorithms that organizations use. The formulas may be more complex than our equation for a straight line, but modern software handles this complexity for the data analyst. So, in general, most algorithms are generally created by "training" them on historical data. The resulting model is then deployed to a business system and the algorithm is fed data it has never seen before. The output of the formula is often referred to as a score, which is simply a probability or likelihood that something is going to happen. This probability could be the likelihood that a transaction is fraud, the probability that you will click on an offer from a website, or the likelihood that your equipment will break down. Figure 2.3 (adapted from *Predictive Analytics: The Power to Predict Who Will Click, Buy, Lie, or Die* by Eric Siegel) is a conceptual illustration of how predictive analytics works and how it can be used to make a business decision.

Figure 2.3: Predictive Analytics in Action

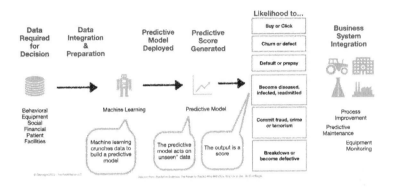

Prescriptive Analytics: What Should We Do?

The last pillar of our analytic categories is prescriptive analytics, which connects the insight to action. At its core, prescriptive analytics involves techniques and methods designed to answer the question "**What should we do?**" We see prescriptive analytics in everyday life as well.

To illustrate the concept of prescriptive analytics, we need not look further than the maps on our smartphone. When you need driving directions somewhere, you simply type in the address and the phone will provide directions on how to get there. It prescribes the route you should take based on your settings, generally by fastest time or shortest route. If there is an accident or traffic jam ahead, some apps even reroute you in real time. Others tell you to slow down so you don't get a speeding ticket because there is a cop close by.

Another great example of prescriptive analytics is a recommendation engine. We see this frequently as well. An example would be a recommendation on what to watch from popular streaming services like Netflix or what you should buy or bundle with an order from Amazon.

AI Defined

For many, confusion about AI stems from there not being really one universally accepted definition of artificial intelligence. The research and advisory firm Gartner provides the following definition of AI: "Artificial intelligence (AI) applies advanced analysis and logic-based techniques, including machine learning, to interpret events, support and automate decisions, and take action."

Figure 2.4 identifies a few historical definitions of AI.[1]

Figure 2.4: Historical Definitions of Artificial Intelligence

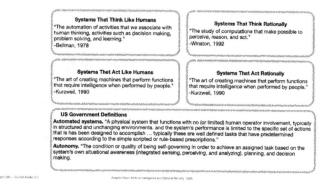

To recap, AI is often segmented into two categories:

- **Artificial General Intelligence** (AGI), also referred to as "strong AI" or "general AI."

- **Artificial Narrow Intelligence** (ANI), also referred to as "narrow AI."

Narrow AI is in extensive use today and is applicable to every industry and business function. Moving forward, we will simply refer to Narrow AI as "AI." It is simply a set of technologies that can be used to solve specific problems.

For our purposes, we will define AI as the following:

Data + Analytic insights + Automation = AI

AI, Machine Learning, and Deep Learning

There are many terms that are bantered about in the data science world. Of particular note is the relationship between AI, machine learning, and deep learning. Figure 2.5 highlights the relationship between the three.

Figure 2.5: Relationship Between AI, ML, and Deep Learning

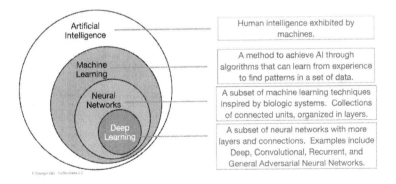

AI Patterns and Use Cases

AI can be applied to a wide variety of use cases. Below are a few examples of the tasks it can solve.

Playing Games

AI is increasingly being used for game playing that requires strategy and "human intelligence":

- **IBM Watson** defeating "Jeopardy" champions Ken Jennings and Brad Ritter in February 2011.[2]
- **Google's DeepMind AlphaGo** defeating an 18-time world "Go" champion in March 2016.[3]
- **Sony, Microsoft, Electronic Arts,** and many others are "investigating the use of reinforcement-learning in game AI agents that can collaborate with human players."[4]

In addition to the above, AI is increasingly being used in game development for non-player characters.

Pattern Recognition and Anti-Pattern Recognition (e.g., Anomalies)

- **Mortgage lenders** discovered that high rates of defaulted mortgages were a result of the sales compensation structure for lending officers.[5]
- **Proctor & Gamble** deployed a solution called "Neighborhood Analytics" that allowed for an understanding of how consumers shopped at a local level. The "Smart Selling" initiative gave P&G insight into what distributors were doing and the ability to then shift resources to prevent stockouts.[6]
- **Xcel Energy**, a large energy provider in the Midwest, partnered with the National Center for Atmospheric Research to provide more accurate wind forecasts. This reduced the margin of error of forecasts by 40%, resulting in $60M in cost reductions for customers and saved millions of tons of carbon

emissions annually due to the lessening of reliance on coal and gas.[7]

- Using computer vision, an **AI named "Mirai"** is able to "predict nearly half of all incidence of breast cancer up to five years before they happen."[8]

- **BMW** is using AI to help improve paint quality on vehicles. "The company states that data from sensors and surface inspections enables over 160 features relating to the car body to be monitored and the quality of the paint application can be predicted very accurately."[9]

- **GEICO** is automating insurance claims by analyzing pictures of damaged cars sent by mechanics. It estimates that 70% of claims can be automated.[10] Unlike other insurers, GEICO is using the AI technology to verify submitted claims on the back-end rather than providing an original estimate itself.

Text Analytics

- **Bank of America** launched a chatbot named "Erica" in 2018. In the first quarter of 2021, it had over 19.5 million clients, 105.6 million interactions, and over 250 million questions answered. And the greatest part: Erica can respond to more than a million unique financial questions.[11]

- **DBS Bank** offers an AI named "JIM" (Job Intelligence Maestro) that reviews resumes, collects responses to screening questions, answers candidate questions, and conducts profiling assessments—all in real-time, 24 hours a day. This saves DBS Bank about 40 human-hours per month. It also developed an employee attrition model that uses data like training, compensation, and leave patterns to predict if an employee will quit the organization.[12,13]

- **Domino's Pizza** allows anyone to order from a variety of platforms, including Facebook, Twitter, Amazon Alexa, Google Home, Slack, Facebook Messenger, Ford Sync, Samsung Smart TV, text messages, and smartwatches. Favorite items can also be saved and the AI then fills orders autonomously. Bots can remember customers' addresses and payment details as well.[14]

Summary

As you can see, AI is used across a variety of use cases. We examined the different categories of analytics (descriptive through prescriptive) and provided a pragmatic definition of AI. We shared how AI, ML, and deep learning were related and then examined usage patterns of AI. The common ones are game playing, pattern and anti-pattern recognition, computer vision, and text analytics.

Chapter 2 References

1   "Artificial Intelligence and National Security." Congressional Research Service (CRS). November 10, 2020. https://crsreports.congress.gov/product/pdf/R/R45178.

2   "IBM100: A Computer Called Watson." IBM Corporation. March 7, 2012. https://www.ibm.com/ibm/history/ibm100/us/en/icons/watson/.

3   DeepMind. "AlphaGo: The Story So Far." DeepMind. 2016. https://deepmind.com/research/case-studies/alphago-the-story-so-far.

4   Stuart, Keith. "Think, Fight, Feel: How Video Game Artificial Intelligence Is Evolving." Guardian. July 19, 2021. https://www.theguardian.com/games/2021/jul/19/video-gaming-artificial-intelligence-ai-is-evolving.

5 Duffy, Nigel, and Karsten Füser. "Six Ways the CFO Can Use Artificial Intelligence, Today." EY. September 19, 2019. https://www.ey.com/en_us/ai/six-ways-the-cfo-can-use-artificial-intelligence-today.

6 "For Procter & Gamble, Data Is at the Heart of Digital Transformation." Microsoft Customers Stories. August 17, 2021. https://customers.microsoft.com/en-us/story/1402016901008352804-procter-and-gamble-consumer-goods-azure.

7 TOMB2020. "Xcel Energy: Utilizing Machine Learning to Efficiently and Reliably Incorporate Renewable Energy into the U.S. Energy Grid; Technology and Operations Management." Technology and Operations Management. November 13, 2018. https://digital.hbs.edu/platform-rctom/submission/xcel-energy-utilizing-machine-learning-to-efficiently-and-reliably-incorporate-renewable-energy-into-the-u-s-energy-grid/.

8 Zeitchik, Steven. "Is Artificial Intelligence about to Transform the Mammogram?" Washington Post, December 21, 2021. https://www.washingtonpost.com/technology/2021/12/21/mammogram-artificial-intelligence-cancer-prediction/.

9 Farish, Mike. "AI Data Analytics for the Paintshop." Automotive Manufacturing Solutions. December 17, 2021. https://www.automotivemanufacturingsolutions.com/bmw/ai-data-analytics-for-the-paintshop/42584.article.

10 Huetter, John. "GEICO to Use Tractable AI Review to Double-Check Estimates." Repairer Driven News. May 27, 2021. https://www.repairerdrivennews.com/2021/05/27/geico-to-use-tractable-ai-to-double-check-estimates/.

11 Schwartz, Eric. "Bank of America's Virtual Assistant Erica Explodes in Popularity." Voicebot.ai. April 21, 2021. https://voicebot.ai/2021/04/21/bank-of-americas-virtual-assistant-erica-explodes-in-popularity/.

12 "Creating Jim, SEA's First Recruitment Chatbot." DBS Innovates. November 1, 2018. https://www.dbs.com/innovation/dbs-innovates/creating-jim-southeast-asias-first-recruitment-chatbot.html.

13 Bean, Randy, and Thomas H. Davenport. "Portrait of an AI Leader: Piyush Gupta of DBS Bank." MIT Sloan Management Review. August 31, 2021. https://sloanreview.mit.edu/article/portrait-of-an-ai-leader-piyush-gupta-of-dbs-bank/.

14 "Domino's Anyware." Domino's Anyware. 2013. https://anyware.dominos.com/.

Chapter 3

How Does AI Work?

In Chapter 2 we provided a definition of AI, discussed the four different types of AI use cases, and gave some practical examples of how AI is used across various industries. In this chapter, we'll provide a brief introduction to the different data, analytics, and automation technologies that comprise AI.

Data Is the Foundation for AI

Without data, there is no AI, and data is growing in complexity. There are different categories, types, and formats that can be at rest or in motion. Data can be internal or external—in the cloud or on premise. You may own and control the data used by AI or you may buy, rent, or lease it from a third party.

Whatever its form, data is the foundation and raw ingredient for AI.

On its own, data is inert—it doesn't react or do anything. Applying analytics and automaton to data increases its value and makes it transformative.

Data is pervasive; data is everywhere; the trick is finding the signal through the noise. But before we can do that, we must first discuss the categories, types, and modern practices of data.

Categories of Data

There are many types of data that can be used for your AI applications. This is by no means exhaustive list:

- **Behavioral** data describes the actions of users or customers. It's generally collected through products and services. It may include website analytics, app usage, button clicks, search data, cursor tracking, eye tracking, facial expressions, and physical interactions.

- **Biometric** data represents a person's physical features and characteristics. This could include input from an eye or face scan, fingerprint, or even someone's voice. Biometrics is commonly used for determining the identity of a person logging onto a smartphone or app.

- **Climate** data is about the weather. In the United States, the National Oceanic and Atmospheric Administration (NOAA) provides access to "quality controlled daily, monthly, seasonal, and yearly measurements of temperature, precipitation, wind and degree days as well as radar data and 30-year Climate Normals."[1]

- **Demographic** data describes people. It includes socioeconomic information such as gender, age, ethnicity, home ownership, income level, smartphone ownership, etc.

- **Firmographic** data is similar to demographic, except it's used to categorize organizations instead of people. This may be geographic area; number of clients; type of organization, industry, technology, or ownership (e.g., public or private); total sales and revenue; etc.

- **Genomic** data tracks the DNA of organisms. It is commonly used to improve the health and well-being of people and may be used to diagnose diseases, prescribe treatment regimens, and even prevent diseases.

- **Geospatial** data describes objects, events, features, or phenomena that have a location on the earth.

- **Machine** data, also known as log data, is generated from applications and computer programs. It is generally a time-stamped series of events that occur when the program is running.

- **Reference** data is standardized information that is governed by a set of rules. This may be currency codes, country names, state abbreviations, etc.

- **Transactional** data is the most common type in an organization. It's collected through sales of goods and services (transactions), production data (if you're a manufacturer), or trip data (if you are Lyft or Uber).

This list could go on and on, but as you can see it is only a small sample data types that can exist in an organization. Depending on your AI project, you may use one or all these. The key is to make sure that the data is unbiased, of sufficient quality, trustworthiness, and availability when needed at runtime.

Data Types and Formats

Now that we understand the categories of data that may exist, let's examine different types that may be available for your business. Data types include:

- **Audio** data can be captured from microphones, smartphones, and home devices like Alexa, Siri, and Google Home. It can be used for speech recognition, customer satisfaction, media content analysis, and equipment monitoring.

- **Categorical** data is more of an organizational method, with information being stored in groups. This data may represent characteristics of a person's gender, marital status, or be calculated from numeric data like fraud/not-fraud or yes/no.

- **Image** data could include pictures, scanned documents, satellite images, and aerial photographs.

- **Numeric** data is straightforward, denoting numbers. These could be SKUs, transaction amounts, temperatures, pressures, voltages, speeds, payment amounts, etc.

- **Streaming** data is continually generated by a source system, which is a continuous flow of data and can be generated from a car, agricultural equipment, machinery, smartphone, or user behavior from other such devices.

- **Text** data is words, sentences, and phrases. It can be mined from legal documents, healthcare information, maintenance logs, invoices, social media, and chatbots.

- **Video** data can be captured from smartphones, security cameras, movies, and TV shows. It can be used for fraud detection, media recommendations, and user authentication.

Modern Data Management

Historically, traditional data management techniques involved extracting data from a few source systems, such as enterprise resource planning (ERP), customer relationship management (CRM), or a manufacturing execution system (MES). An IT team would then standardize, integrate, transform, and store it in an enterprise data warehouse (EDW) that was useful for the business. This process is known as ETL (extract, transform, and load). The data would also be secured and governed. In many cases, downstream business intelligence (BI) applications would then access the data to produce standardized reports. When the business needed to answer a new question or underlying business conditions changed, the original data model needed to change. Unfortunately, changing it was time consuming and expensive. Additionally, most data management was done in batch. For an organization to be truly AI-driven, modern data management practices are needed.

The key requirements for data teams include:

- **Connecting and combining data from disparate data sources**. For many businesses, data is no longer contained onsite and is distributed across geographic regions; some of it on premise, some in the cloud. There are a dizzying array of formats and types, and some data sets are streaming while others are at rest.

- **Less batch, more real-time.** Simply stated, batch data processing is of a bygone era. If your organization is relying heavily on it, you will not have the flexibility and adaptability needed for the modern world. Organizations need to be able to process data in real-time or near real-time so the correct insights can be delivered to the right employee, partner, customer, or system at the right time. If you are relying on dated, inflexible batch processes, you will not be able to move at the speed of digital.

- **More self-service**. In the past, experts in IT organizations usually practiced data management. They had a standard way of approaching change. We still need this. However, IT today can't work in isolation. Technical entity relationship (ER) diagrams are no longer sufficient for the business. Users find them too hard to interpret and need to have a catalog of data sources, an understanding of the context of the data, where it originated, how it was collected, what calculations and transformations were completed, and what the columns mean.

- **Cloud-centric**. Modern data ecosystems require a cloud-first approach with data persisting in a cloud **data lake**. This is a centralized repository that allows organizations to store any data type (structured or unstructured) at any scale. All the hyper-scalers (Amazon, Google, Microsoft) have data lakes. The cloud allows organizations to increase or decrease capacity on demand. The major difference between a data lake and a data warehouse is in the structure. A **data lake** is simply a dumping ground of raw, unfiltered data, whereas a **data warehouse** has been refined and contains structure for a particular purpose. An example would be a data warehouse that has been created for businesses to generate reports and dashboards.

- **Common metadata**. Metadata is essentially data about data. This may sound a bit strange but think about it like this: If you take picture with your smartphone, the data is the image or picture. What info does your camera store about the picture? Well, metadata includes the date and time the picture was taken, the type of camera used, the number of megapixels, the pixel size of the image, the storage size of the image, the picture format, and so forth. Why is this important? Because a data lake is messy—organizations just dump data into it. Metadata provides organizations the ability to understand what data exists in their organization. Think of it like a card catalog for a library or your playlist. In addition to knowing what exists, metadata provides lineage or providence of the data (required if you need to explain how an AI decision was made), its quality, size, when it was last updated, how it may connect and integrate with other data, and a description of what it is.

- **Built-in quality and trust**. Businesses are dynamic and constantly changing. The IT team needs to provide quality and trustworthy data to a business. When AI makes decisions, it has the power to impact large populations of people—both positively and negatively. Organizations need to ensure it is understood who has access to the data and there should be strict controls in managing sensitive or protected information. With conventions like General Data Protection Regulation (GDPR) in the European Union or the California Consumer Privacy Act (CCPA) in the United States, individuals have more control and rights over their personal data. Business and IT teams need to be able to satisfy these requirements. For example, under both the CCPA and GDPR, users now have the right to be forgotten. This means you essentially can request your data to be deleted. So, if you make this request to an entity, it needs to be able to make that happen.

Does your organization have the right foundational elements for a modern data stack? This is the foundation from which all AI will follow. Now that we have a basic understanding of data categories, types, and modern data management principles, we will turn our attention to AI technologies.

AI Technologies

In Chapter 1, we defined AI as a fusion of data, analytics, and automation technologies. In this section, we'll provide a brief introduction to the different technologies commonly used. This is not intended to make you an expert but rather to provide a working understanding of current technologies and how they're applied. This is illustrated in Figure 3.1.

Figure 3.1: A Pragmatic Definition of AI

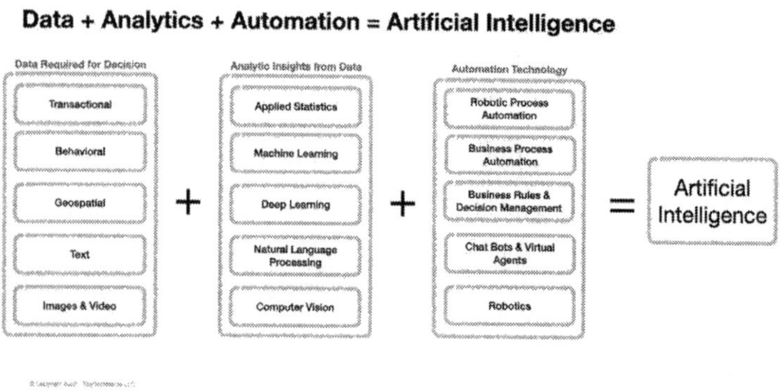

Data + Analytics + Automation = Artificial Intelligence

Please note this is not an exhaustive compendium of all the different technologies and techniques used by AI. Technologies like mathematical optimization, automated scheduling, and hardware like GPUs are not covered in this book. If they were, it wouldn't be a TinyTechGuide!

Generally speaking, there are five broad problem types for which AI is deployed. They are regression, classification, clustering, natural language processing (NLP), and computer vision.

- **Regression** methods predict a numerical outcome like payment amount, yield, or product sales.

- **Classification** algorithms predict a categorical outcome such as fraud/not fraud or to admit/not-admit a patient to the emergency room.

- **Clustering** techniques organize groups of unlabeled data together. This is commonly used for customer segmentation. In other words, the objects in the same cluster are more similar to one another than objects in a different cluster.

- **Natural language processing (NLP)** turns text or audio speech into structured information. This can be used to understand sentiment and emotions.

- **Computer vision** is a set of techniques that capture, process, and analyze images and videos. This allows computers to extract meaningful, contextual information from the physical world. It can be used to improve manufacturing quality, detect anomalies in medical images, or determine whether someone is wearing a face mask.

The most popular algorithms in use today can be seen in Figure 3.2.[2]

Figure 3.2: Most Popular Analytic Techniques

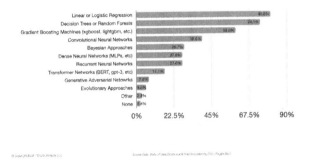

Types of Machine Learning

For machine learning, there are generally three types of methodologies: supervised learning, unsupervised learning, and reinforcement learning. Now, one should note that there are lots of other algorithm types and methodologies that include semi-supervised learning, deep learning techniques, and algorithms for feature selection, optimization, computer vision, natural language processing, and many others. My goal here is not to provide an exhaustive list of techniques or algorithms, but rather an introduction to the major algorithm categories, sample algorithm names, and approaches applied to solve a specific set of business problems. Figure 3.3 illustrates the major types of machine learning.

Figure 3.3: Types of Machine Learning

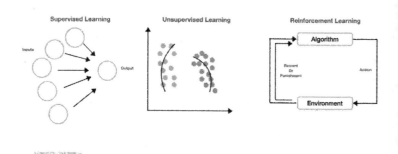

Supervised Learning

These are a class of algorithms that use training data to learn how the inputs (also known as predictors, variables, or features) are related to the outputs (also known as the outcome or response). If your historical data has an outcome (the thing you want to predict), this is often referred to as labeled data. For example, if you want to predict the creditworthiness of an individual, you may provide the algorithm with historical data that has inputs (e.g., types of accounts, income level, payment history, credit utilization rate, length of history, rent and utility payments, etc.) and a categorical variable flag that tells you if this person were a good or bad credit risk.

Table 3.1 highlights specific supervised learning algorithm types, methods, and example use cases. The sample algorithms are only listed so you need not be scared if you hear these words from data analysts or data scientists. As previously mentioned, this is not an exhaustive list—there are plenty of other readily available resources that will cover methods, when to use what, and why. Also, it should be noted that the example use cases might be applicable across many of the different algorithm types.

Table 3.1: Supervised ML Algorithm Types, Methods, and Example Use Cases

Types	Samples	Example Use Cases
Bayesian Algorithms: Based on Bayes Theorem that states that the probability of an event can be calculated based on awareness of factors (prior probabilities) that might affect the event.	• Naive bayes • Gaussian naive bayes • Bayesian networks	**Spam filtering:** Is this email spam? **Sentiment analysis:** Is this customer feedback positive or negative? **Agriculture:** What will my crop yield be this year?

Types	Samples	Example Use Cases
Decision Trees **Classification (or regression models)**: Split each variable or feature into a new branch. The output is essentially a set of if-then rules that are easily interpretable.	• Classification and regression tree (CART) • C4.5 and C5.0 • Chi-squared automatic interaction detection (CHAID)	**Healthcare**: What are the risk factors for depression? **Banking**: How likely is a mortgage applicant to default on their payments? **Manufacturing**: What were the top factors causing the machine to fail?
Deep Learning: Larger and more complex neural networks that are commonly used for voice, video, and image analysis.	• Convolutional neural networks (CNN) • Recurrent neural networks (RNNs) • Autoencoders	**Insurance**: Given the images uploaded from the claimant, does the repair estimate correlate to the damage? **Consumer**: Given a grainy picture, can we used AI to enhance its quality? **Voice search**: How does Alexa, Siri, or Google Assistant translate my speech to text?

Types	Samples	Example Use Cases
Ensemble Methods: Create many models independently that are combined to make a single, stronger model. Think "wisdom of the crowds."	• Random forests • AdaBoost • Gradient boosting machines	**Supply chain**: Determining the tiers of a supply chain when information is not shared. **Insurance**: What should we set our insurance rates at? **Finance**: Is this company committing fraud by manipulating financial statements?
Neural Networks: Modeled after the human brain, neural networks—also known as artificial neural networks (ANNs)—have a set of inputs, with one or more hidden layers (neurons), then an output.	• Perceptron • Stochastic gradient descent • Back-propagation	**Logistics**: When are my shipments expected to arrive? **HR**: Is this candidate likely to succeed in this role? **Sales & Marketing**: What is the lead quality score for this prospect?

Types	Samples	Example Use Cases
Regression: Classic, explainable (interpretable) modeling technique that finds best-fit linear relationships between the inputs (independent variables) and outputs (dependent variable).	• Linear regression • Logistic regression • Stepwise regression • Multivariate adaptive regression splines (MARS)	**Insurance:** Is this applicant a good or bad insurance risk? **Real estate:** What should the appraisal of this property be? **Healthcare:** What is the likelihood of disease or death given the patient's historical data?
Support Vector Machines: Most commonly used for classification problems (but can be used for regression problems), the algorithm defines a line or hyperplane that best divides a data set into two classes or categories.	• Linear SVM • Polynomial function (PF) • Gaussian radial basis function (RBF)	**Security:** Is this person or object a threat (image classification)? **Shipping:** What zip code do these handwritten digits correspond to? **Consumer goods:** Can I unlock my smartphone with my face (facial recognition)?

Unsupervised Learning

These algorithms are used when you do not have labels on your data. Essentially, the computer figures out patterns in it. A common example is clustering, where you insert the data and the algorithms group "like" points together. A common use case of clustering is for customer segmentation, which puts customers with similar attributes or buying behaviors into the same group. Table 3.2 provides examples of unsupervised ML algorithm types, methods, and use cases.

Table 3.2: Unsupervised ML Algorithm Types, Methods, and Example Use Cases

Types	Samples	Example Use Cases
Association Rules: Rubrics for discovering patterns between items in large transactional data sets.	• Apriori • FP-growth • MaxEclat	**Market Basket Analysis**: What items are purchased together? **Medical diagnosis**: What relationships exist between symptoms and illness? **E-commerce**: What web page are you likely to visit next?

Types	Samples	Example Use Cases
Clustering: Group data or objects together based on similarities.	• K-means • Hierarchical clustering • Density-based spatial clustering of applications with noise (DBSCAN)	**Segmentation**: Which customers are similar to one another based on buying behavior? **Image classification**: Can we group our like-product images together? **Urban planning**: Can we detect urban clusters based on ride share and social check in data?

Reinforcement Learning

These are a class of algorithms that learn through trial and error. Essentially, using simulations, they play a "game" millions of times. Reinforcement learning algorithms (RLs) use a system of rewards and/or punishments to train the algorithm. To illustrate how a RL works in practice, think of the classic game of Frogger.

Frogger is a simple game. Generally, there is a road or highway, and the frog must cross the road to earn points. The vehicles move left to right (x-direction) and the frog can move in all directions (x direction, as well as the y direction, up and down). If the Frogger gets hit by a vehicle, you lose—game over!

Using reinforcement learning (RL) to teach a computer how to play Frogger is quite simple. If the Frog gets hit by a car, the RL algorithm is penalized -1 point, and if it finds a present, the Frogger is rewarded with +1 point. Unity makes a video game development platform. It posted an excellent YouTube video on teaching a computer to play Frogger using RL.[3]

It did this via simulation. Essentially, the computer was allowed to play the game over and over so it could "learn the rules." After six hours of training (millions of simulations), a super Frogger had been created. It scooped up all the presents in record time—all by learning on its own, without human involvement!

Danny Lange, Unity computer scientist who has led AI teams at Uber, Amazon, Microsoft, and IBM described some interesting emergent behavior. Why did the Frogger move "forward" to find presents? It could have just as easily gone backwards. Essentially, this emergent behavior results from the rewards function that is used in the AI system. If you're not careful, you could have some unwanted behaviors and unanticipated consequences from your AI system.

Now, the Frogger example was interesting, but this is the same way robots and self-driving cars are trained. It all starts with a simulated environment. If the car or robot hits something or veers off course, then -1 point, game over. The simulation starts over and this process recurs millions and billions of times.

Natural Language Technology

Another key technology component of AI are natural language technologies (NLTs). The ML algorithms covered in the previous section have fueled the adoption and usage of natural language technologies, which allow humans and computers to interact in a much more natural way than the input/output of a keyboard. Whether you have Amazon Alexa, Google Home, or another smart device, it's easier to talk and receive information from the machine with an intuitive format. Key technologies include chatbots and virtual assistants, natural language processing (NLP), natural language generation (NLG), natural language understanding (NLU), machine translation, intelligent document processing (IDP), speech analytics, text analytics, text-to-speech technology.

NLP and Text Analytics

Natural language processing (NLP) involves the ability to turn text or audio speech into encoded, structured information based on an appropriate organizational configuration. The structured data may be used simply to classify a document, as in "this report describes a laparoscopic cholecystectomy," or it may be used to identify findings, procedures, medications, allergies, and participants.[4]

Text analytics is an umbrella term used to describe the process of extracting usable insight from unstructured data. It may be used to categorize or summarize text, extract entities, and detect emotions or sentiment contained within text data. Organizations may use this to monitor social media feeds, detect adverse medical reactions from social media, extract contract terms, determine brand loyalty, and many other use cases.

NLG

Natural language generation (NLG) is commonly used in business intelligence (BI) reporting and dashboarding tools. Structured and unstructured data is used to construct sentences and phrases forming a narrative based on the data. Examples of this are seeing a trend chart and overlaid on it is a reason why the chart went up or down in your native language. You may see these as autogenerated interpretations of your stock portfolio funds or credit card statements.

A couple of examples include the **Orlando Magic basketball team** using NLG to customize communications and email to consumers for a hyper-personalized experience.[5] NLG is also used to write data-driven sports stories.[6] For example, Yahoo! Sports uses NLG to create over 70 million different reports and recaps.[7]

NLU

Natural language understanding is a subset of NLP. The goal of NLU is to understand what the natural language input is ultimately trying to do. Think about it as interpreting the natural language.

Machine Translation

Machine translation is used to convert text from one language to another. A great example of this is Google Translate. You can type any phrase and have it translated to any other language instantaneously.

Intelligent Document Processing (IDP)

Intelligent document processing uses computer vision to extract data from unstructured text documents. Whether you're trying to extract text data from receipts, invoices, maintenance records, medical claims, shipping forms, tax documents, or PDFs, IDP is the technology that makes it happen. It really removes the tedium that human reviewers would endure doing this repetitive work.

Text to Speech

Text to speech is the automatic extraction of natural language from recorded and voice streams. Every time you talk to your phone to search Google, it is using text-to-speech technology to transform your words into text that the computer can understand. This can be used in conversational applications like call centers to monitor conversations and agents' performance. Due to the pandemic, we're seeing more of this in everyday business via the automatic transcription of meetings with Zoom or Microsoft Teams.

Figure 3.4 provides an overview of natural language technologies.

Figure 3.4: Natural Language Technologies

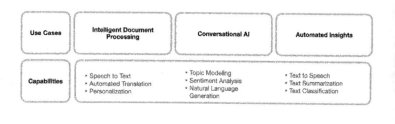

Computer Vision

Computer vision is AI that uses machine learning and deep learning to make sense of videos, pictures, and images. It is commonly used for facial recognition, image recognition, video analytics, and text extraction.

Facial Recognition

Facial recognition is a specialized form of object detection and classification where the object is a human face. It may be able to identify the face outright; the features of the face like eyes, nose, mouth, and hair color; and whether the person is smiling or not.

Image Classification

Image classification is used to organize a group of images into a set of categories or classes with a set of training images. Think hot dog/not hot dog.

Object Detection and Segmentation

If an image has more than one element, object detection tries to identify each one by using a set of bounding boxes. Image segmentation attempts to identify each of the sub-parts or sub-objects in each segment. As an example, if you took an image of a car, it may recognize the tires, license plate, windshield, and other components.

Video Analytics

Video analytics evaluates moving objects. This involves detecting objects, segmenting them, and tracking their trajectory.

Optical Character Recognition (OCR)

This is the process of reading text from images using computer vision and NLP.

Automation Technologies

Robotic Process Automation

Robotic process automation (RPA) is software allowing organizations to build scripts that emulate what a human office worker would do when completing a specific task. It executes a workflow that can integrate with any application that has a user interface. With RPA, organizations can set up the system to have a human in the loop (attended) or be completely autonomous and automatic (unattended). With attended RPA, a bot acts like a virtual assistant to the employee, with the bot creating an "augmented analyst" that works "side by side" with the human.

RPA allows companies to automate tedious, manual, repetitive tasks. Bots, also known as digital workers, can understand what is on a screen, input keystrokes, do mouse clicks, extract data, and perform a predefined set of actions. Some have referred to RPA bots as digital assistants. Many RPA software vendors have a dashboard that allows customers to deploy and manage thousands or tens of thousands of bots across an organization.

For example, in the accounting department, RPA can be used to send incoming invoices to the next person for approval or automate the PO-matching process and check for errors before submitting any payments.

Business Process Automation

In contrast to RPAs, business process automation (BPA) is used to program a sequence of tasks that would form a particular business process. Essentially, BPA automates a workflow and triggers the next step of the process as soon as the previous step is completed. Although similar in nature, RPA generally automates one specific task, while BPA automates a multi-step process. From an implementation perspective, RPA can be executed with a low-code/no-code platform and BPA is generally more complex. BPA is part of a broader business process management (BPM) that is more holistic in nature and is meant to automate an entire end-to-end process.

Chatbots and Virtual Assistants

Chatbots and virtual assistants are commonly used in the customer service industries and can be transformative for organizations. They help automate repetitive tasks that normally would require a human. For example, if you need to update your mailing address for your credit card statement or healthcare provider, check an order status, or open/close an account, you commonly accomplish this via a chatbot.

Business Rules and Decision Management

Decision management is another form of automation that focuses on computerizing business decisions. These generally combine business rules, machine learning, and optimization to make decisions and trigger actions. Additionally, these solutions often operate on streaming data. These are generally used for operationalizing decisions.

Robotics

Robots are used to automate repetitive physical tasks. We often see them used in warehousing operations. For example, Amazon uses them to help reduce the manual repetitive task of its employees in warehouses. The robots named Bert and Ernie are used to move items across fulfillment centers.[8] Not only does this improve efficiency and operations, but Amazon claims it also has the potential to reduce safety-related incidents.

AI Ops

As organizations embed AI throughout business operations, particular attention must be paid to the models that are deployed. Deploying AI is very different than deploying other types of software.

How Is AI Different?

When organizations deploy typical software—if it's on-premise software—it's installed and configured and users are generally assigned permissions that allow them to access specific functionality. As companies migrate to cloud software there is a similar process, but a third party handles software maintenance and operation.

As an example, if you look at an HR software package like Workday, CRM system like Salesforce, or accounting software like Intuit QuickBooks, once the software is installed and configured, it simply works. IT teams will certainly monitor it to make sure it's running as designed but it doesn't take a lot of TLC (tender loving care). There may be bug fixes and upgrades, but the organization doesn't really need to think about it.

Now, if we think about AI systems, these are underpinned by different types of data and ML models. If you recall from Chapter 2, models are generally trained on historical data, which fundamentally represented a state of the world at a specific point in time. The model was tested and validated, then deployed or embedded within a business system.

What happens when the world changes? For example, when the COVID-19 pandemic first started, it broke everyone's models.[9] Why? Because consumer habits changed. The everyday patterns of life were disrupted so the assumptions that were used to create the models in the first place were no longer valid. Essentially, the new data that was fed into the analytic models was very different than the original training data and predictions coming out of the models were suboptimal.

To deal with the complexity of AI systems, Gartner has coined the term XOps as an umbrella term for DataOps, ModelOps, and DevOps.[10] XOps is a set of practices that use automation technologies, repeatable processes, and best practices to ensure economies of scale across IT systems. This is illustrated in Figure 3.5.

Figure 3.5: XOps Framework

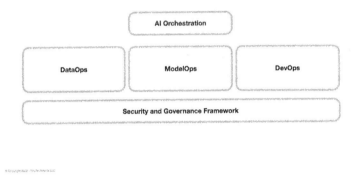

DataOps

DataOps, or data operationalization, is a set of practices, processes, architectural patterns, and procedures that aim to accelerate the integration and automation of data management workflows (aka pipelines) across the organization. One of the goals of DataOps is to improve collaboration from data engineers, data scientists, and IT developers.

ModelOps

Since the real world is constantly changing, data that models use is constantly changing. Businesses need to invest in ModelOps.

> *ModelOps [MLOps] is a cross-functional, collaborative, continuous process that focuses on operationalizing data science by managing statistical, data science, and machine learning models as reusable, highly available software artifacts, via a repeatable deployment process. It encompasses unique management aspects that span model inference, scalability, maintenance, auditing, and governance, as well as the ongoing monitoring of models in production to ensure they are still delivering positive business value as the underlying conditions change."*[11]

There are many facets to ModelOps but a core component is model monitoring and updates.

Model Monitoring

When organizations deploy models in a production system, constant monitoring is required to ensure that performance meets expectations. If not, models need to be replaced or updated. There are a variety of metrics that can be used to monitor performance but business metrics, model metrics, and IT metrics should be included.

- **Business metrics** evaluate how the model is impacting business results. For example, imagine you are buying display ads on a website. You're spending money but is this achieving the desired results? Are you getting the click through and conversion rates that you anticipated?

- **Performance metrics** are what IT looks at quite closely. These may include the number of records scored, input/output metrics, execution times, and CPU usage.

- **Model metrics** are designed to understand how your model is performing and often segmented into three broad categories:

  - **Accuracy** gauges how well your model is performing. Data scientists track things like confidence rates, error rates, and misclassification rates to evaluate model performance. If the accuracy is not satisfactory, you can update or replace the model with a newer version.

  - **Champion-challenger** is a method to continually find a better model. Essentially, you have a production model (champion) running. In parallel or periodically, you simultaneously test a different model (challenger). If the results of the challenger are better, you can swap it in.

  - **Population stability** is testing new data sets to ensure they are similar to those used to train the models. If the shape and behavior of the data is drastically different, it may be a sign to update or replace the model.

As previously mentioned, models need to be constantly monitored when used in production systems. As the real-world data changes, this is called **data drift** or **model drift**. For example, imagine looking at predictions for a restaurant's online orders prior to the COVID-19 pandemic. You may have models to set prices and offer promotions based on certain real-world conditions. After COVID-19, all the consumer buying behaviors patterns changed. Supply chains changed. Everything changed. Organizations need to closely monitor their models, using the aforementioned metrics, and not assume they are behaving as designed. If the model begins to perform sub-optimally, then you need to retrain or build a new one and deploy it back into your business system.

DevOps

Similar to DataOps and ModelOps, DevOps was also designed to increase the productivity of IT teams. DevOps can be considered the first XOps practice. DataOps and ModelOps came after DevOps.

Essentially, DevOps is a set of practices, policies, tools, and philosophies that allow an organization to deliver applications and services at scale. Core tenants of DevOps include cross-team collaboration. As an example, developers, security teams, and software quality teams may be combined to deliver services and apps to the business. DevOps allow for accelerated delivery, improved reliability, heightened collaboration, and scaling for an organization.

Summary

In this chapter, we provided an overview of the different types of ML technologies. We discussed supervised, unsupervised, and reinforcement learning techniques. We then discussed natural language technologies, including NLP, NLG, and NLU. We also examined computer vision and automation technologies like robotic process automation. Lastly, we discussed the importance of AIOps, including DataOps, ModelOps, and DevOps to create a comprehensive framework that organizations can use to accelerate the delivery of AI applications.

Chapter 3 References

1   "2021 Gartner Hype Cycle for Natural Language Technologies." Uniphore. October 14, 2021. https://www.

uniphore.com/research/2021-gartner-hype-cycle-for-natural-language-technologies/.

2   "State of Data Science and Machine Learning 2021." Kaggle. 2021. https://www.kaggle.com/kaggle-survey-2021.

3   "Unity Machine Learning: Reinforcement Learning Demo [video]." YouTube. June 30, 2017. https://youtu.be/fiQsmdwEGT8.

4   "Definition of Natural-Language Processing (NLP): Gartner Information Technology Glossary." Gartner. n.d. Accessed January 11, 2022. https://www.gartner.com/en/information-technology/glossary/natural-language-processing-nlp.

5   "Orlando Magic." Automated Insights. n.d. Accessed January 17, 2022. https://automatedinsights.com/customer-stories/orlando-magic/.

6   Arria NLG. "Arria NLG Partners with Sports Analytics Leader, Boost Sport AI to Empower and Ignite Media, Sports Betting and E-Commerce with AI and Data-Driven Natural-Language Content." PR Newswire. May 25, 2021. https://www.prnewswire.com/news-releases/arria-nlg-partners-with-sports-analytics-leader-boost-sport-ai-to-empower-and-ignite-media-sports-betting-and-e-commerce-with-ai-and-data-driven-natural-language-content-301299076.html.

7   "Yahoo!" Automated Insights. n.d. Accessed February 5, 2022. https://automatedinsights.com/customer-stories/yahoo/.

8   Feiner, Lauren. "Amazon Details New Warehouse Robots, 'Ernie' and 'Bert.'" CNBC. June 13, 2021. https://www.cnbc.com/2021/06/13/amazon-details-new-warehouse-robots-ernie-and-bert.html.

9   Burkhardt, Roger, Carlos Fernandez Naveira, Carlo Giovine, and Arvind Govindarajan. "Leadership's Role in Fixing the Analytics Models That COVID-19 Broke." McKinsey. September 1, 2020. https://www.mckinsey.

com/business-functions/mckinsey-analytics/our-insights/
leaderships-role-in-fixing-the-analytics-models-that-covid-19-
broke.

10 Panetta, Kasey. "Gartner Top Data and Analytics Trends for
2021." Gartner. March 15, 2021. https://www.gartner.com/
smarterwithgartner/gartner-top-10-data-and-analytics-trends-
for-2021.

11 Sweenor, David, Steven Hillion, Dan Rope, Dev
Kannabiran, Thomas Hill, and Michael O'Connell. ML Ops:
Operationalizing Data Science. Sebastopol, CA: O'Reilly
Media, 2020. https://www.oreilly.com/
library/view/ml-ops-operationalizing/9781492074663/.

Chapter 4

Who Uses AI?

In Chapter 3, we discussed the different analytics and digital automation technologies used to create artificial intelligence (AI) applications. In this chapter, we'll take a closer look at different examples of how AI is applied across departments and industries. This isn't an exhaustive list and is simply intended to give you a better idea of how businesses use AI in the real world so you can succeed on your AI journey.

AI Across Departments

AI can be applied across every functional area in your organization. In this section I'll show examples of businesses using AI across accounting and finance, marketing and sales, research and development, supply chain, IT, human resources, and service and support.

Accounting and Finance

AI can be used to detect fraud, bad debt, money laundering, and embezzlement, as well as for automating reporting and contract reviews, underwriting, and valuating assets.

Let's look at bad debt first.

Sales Compensation Structure
Leads to Bad Mortgage Debt

Compared to 2019, there was approximately a 26% increase in bad debt in 2020 that cost companies $12,262M.[1] AI can be used to better understand what customers will pay, who may pay late, and who is unlikely to pay at all. One firm employed AI to understand why it had a higher-than-average rate of mortgage defaults. The firm created a predictive model and included typical data like credit worthiness, down payment amount, property value. Then, it combined this with non-traditional data like Salesforce compensation data to train the predictive model. With this it was discovered that certain lending officers had the highest propensity of defaulted mortgages.[2] These mortgage officers were taking advantage of aggressive sales incentives set by the company. After understanding this relationship between compensation structure and bad debt, forecasts of defaults under different scenarios could be created.[3]

Basically, AI was used to detect a link between mortgage officers with high rates of loan defaults and aggressive sales incentives. The firm then acted on this insight to fix its broken compensation structure.

Other examples of AI being used across accounting & finance include:

- **Airbus**, the aerospace company, is using AI to automate its expense management process, through which more than 25,000 travel and expense reports are filed annually. Rather than having a human look at each report and line item, the **AI system automatically examines reports and matches them against a repository of approved vendors and expense types**. The system can examine receipts in more than 100 languages. Now, rather than a human reviewing receipts, the AI does it and only surfaces exceptions. Airbus expects millions of dollars in savings.[4]

- **Equinix**, a real estate investment company, uses optical character recognition (OCR) and robotic process automation (RPA) to improve the **procure-to-pay process**. It automatically extracts data from PDF invoices provided by vendors and only surface the exceptions to an investigation team. This saves over 14,000 hours a year.[5]

- **A global manufacturing company** uses natural language processing (NLP) to scan thousands of leases to **ensure compliance with a new accounting regulation** being implemented.[6]

Marketing and Sales

In marketing and sales, AI is often used for customer service, price optimization, churn identification and reduction, lead scoring and routing, customer segmentation, customer personalization, as well as product and service recommendations.

As an example, let's look at price optimization.

PepsiCo Uses AI to Set Prices and Maximize Revenue

PepsiCo brands include Pepsi, Fritos, Lays, Mountain Dew, Tropicana, Quaker Oats, and Aquafina.[7]

It is using AI to determine **price elasticity**, which is the measure of how much the supply or demand of a product or service changes as the price changes. Being a global brand, PepsiCo operates in over 200 territories and countries and is a $70B company (at the end of 2020). It has 23 global brands that generate over $1B each.[8]

PepsiCo dynamically calculates 40,000 price elasticities. Its Global Senior Vice President Net Revenue Management Colin Lenaghan stated: "If I could give the example, operating with 60 elasticities that help you understand where your pricing opportunity is to 40,000, right? I mean, that's the sort of scale that you're getting to. And then the decomposition of that elasticity around what it drags and draws from across your portfolio, across the portfolio in one retailer versus another retailer, really is sort of mind-blowing around what it can do. And that's a real-life example of a product that we're scaling up as we speak." [9] As PepsiCo continues to refine its AI system prices are increasing and consumers do not seem to mind.[10]

Other examples of marketing and sales using AI include:

- **Starbucks** uses its loyalty program with over 23 million members and Deep Brew AI to personalize offers to patrons and automatically places inventory orders across hundreds of stores in the United States.[11]

- The multinational producer of footwear, athletic apparel, and equipment **Nike, Inc.** uses AI to personalize search and product recommendations. It also uses AI in its supply chain to improve visibility to better understand inventory levels at local and regional levels to ensure products are delivered to the right places at the right time. Lastly, AI is used for product design.[12]

- **JPMorgan Chase** uses AI to create email copy and subject lines, online display ads, and headlines for direct mail.[13] There have been some surprises along the journey. For example, it was discovered: 1) CTAs (calls to action) don't have to be so direct and can be observational, 2) Short ad copy does not relate to ad performance, and 3) The type of language used is different across channels.[14]

Research and Development (R&D)

Many companies use AI to develop products and services. Examples include product configurations and setup, digital twins (virtual models that represent physical objects), product and feature optimization, product or equipment failures, product quality, process optimization, predictive maintenance, and usage.[15,16]

Renault Reduces Time to Development by Half

The design of automated manual transmissions (AMTs) in automobiles can be complex. These systems allow the vehicle to behave like an automatic transmission but empower the driver to shift using a paddle shifter or other push-button system. Since there is a complex electro-mechanical interaction between actuators, gears, sensors, and the status of the vehicle, it can take a year of trial and error to define system requirements. After Renault used software from Siemens, it managed to cut the AMT development time almost in half.[17,18]

Other examples include:

- **Moderna** used **AI and automation to accelerate the mRNA sequencing used to explore potential candidates for vaccines**. With automation and ML algorithms, it increased production capacity from 30 mRNAs per month to about 1,000—with better consistency and quality. This was critical in the development of Moderna's COVID-19 vaccine.[19]

- As **semiconductors** continue to shrink in size, the time and resources it takes to design and manufacture them continues to increase. There are many constraints when laying out a chip: power, frequency, latency, etc. One such **AI system helps to automate and optimize this process**. It can "turn what used to take dozens of engineers weeks or potentially months into something a junior engineer can do on their own in just days."[20]

- **Tyson Foods Inc.** uses **computer vision technology in chicken processing plants to monitor inventory levels and freshness in real time**. The system can identify the product type (stock-keeping unit, SKU), and a scale automatically weighs it. The accuracy is over 90%, which is a 20% improvement over manual processes. The company also invested heavily in robots to accelerate the manufacturing process.[21]

Supply Chain

In supply chain logistics, AI is used for network, inventory, route optimization, sales and parts forecasting, demand planning and forecasting, spend analytics, digital twins, advanced scenario modeling, supplier risk monitoring resolution, and improved supply chain visibility.[22,23]

Companies need to address several difficulties, including:

- Using demand forecasting across multiple geographies and product lines.

- Optimizing supply chain efficiency with constraints and trade-offs with thousands of connected variables.

- Reacting to ever-changing conditions that could affect the manufacturing process, transport of goods, and rapidly evolving consumer habits.

Proctor and Gamble Improves Supply Chain

Proctor and Gamble—the maker of Tide, Cascade, Puffs, and other iconic brands—has always used data and analytics to improve operational excellence. It had plans to use AI to reimagine its supply chain, but the COVID-19 pandemic disrupted those plans.[24] Given the size of the company, it had data in disparate silos and combined them to improve visibility across the supply chain, making it more resilient so the right people could get the right product at the right time. It also moved to a real-time sense-and-respond approach to understand demand, deploying a solution called "Neighborhood Analytics" that allowed an understanding of how consumers shopped at a local level. **The "Smart Selling" initiative gave P&G insight into what distributors were doing and could shift resources to prevent stock outs.**[25]

"For example, Proctor & Gamble uses an AI-enabled digital platform to automate its supply-chain planning, a process that once focused on matching demand with supply over a 30-day period. In today's dynamic supply-chain environment, P&G's planners utilize machine learning (a subfield of AI) algorithms that automatically adjust demand plans for new product launches, changes in stocking strategies, or seasonal shifts. Along with being more productive and accurate, the manufacturer has also freed up its planners to focus on more important tasks." [26]

Other examples include:

- As the pandemic rages on and inflation is on the rise, the retail giant **Walmart** is using AI to optimize inventory management. It uses computer vision and augmented reality (AR) to understand supply levels in storage areas and to direct staff on what to move to the floor. The AR is used to let workers know how to direct the work. It also uses AI to manage inventory levels across millions of SKUs and locations. CEO Doug McMillon said: "We're using ML and AI to do a number of different things. We used it to help adjust to the pandemic and use the stores as fulfillment hubs. And we use it for predictive baskets, smart substitutions. Our in-stock assistant is AI-empowered. We've moved 153 petabytes of data to the cloud so far. And we've got room to grow there. And we can put data and machines to work in ways in this company that we've not yet done, but we are making progress." [27]

- Shipping and logistics company **DHL** uses robotics and computer vision to automatically read shipping manifests and pick and sort packages into delivery bins. Over 1,000 small packages can be sorted per hour with 99% accuracy. This decreases the probability of missorting packages, which increases customer satisfaction.[28]

- Car manufacturer **Audi** is using AI to monitor supplier risk. With a network of over 14,000 suppliers spanning 60 countries, it uses AI to ensure that suppliers adhere to Audi's "Code of Conduct for Business Partners." This contains guidelines and operating principles to ensure its supplier network comply with Audi's requirements for environmental and social responsibility.[29]

Information Technology (IT) Operations

The digital nerve center of many organizations—IT—also uses AI. The term AIOps has emerged to describe the application of AI within IT operations. The research and consulting firm Gartner states: "AIOps combines big data and machine learning to automate IT operations processes, including event correlation, anomaly detection and causality determination."[30]

A few examples include anomaly detection, automated capacity planning (network and infrastructure), cybersecurity, incident prediction, root cause analysis, event correlation, noise reaction, and many others.[31]

American Express Fights Fraud With AI[32]

Cybercrime accounts for 0.8% of worldwide GDP, about $600B annually. This is expected to increase. As the pandemic continues to rage on, consumer habits have shifted and online shopping continues to grow. Financial institutions, credit card companies, and insurance providers are major targets for fraudsters. American Express, with over 115 active credit cards, monitors its transactions in real time. The company is using recurrent neural networks (RNNs) to monitor all those cards and has achieved the lowest fraud rate in the industry for the past 13 years.

Other examples include:

- The **US government** uses AI to combat fraud, waste, and abuse. The Securities and Exchange Commission (SEC), Internal Revenue Service (IRS), and Centers for Medicare and Medicaid Services, and Department of Treasury have many systems in place that use AI.[33]

- **Uber** has developed a system named COTA (Customer Obsession Ticket Assistant) that helps customer service representatives quickly and accurately resolve customer support tickets. COTA uses Uber's Michelangelo-powered models (Uber's machine learning system) to suggest the "three most likely issue types and solutions based on ticket content and trip context."[34]

Human Resources (HR)

People are the lifeblood of every organization and HR departments apply AI across a variety of business processes. AI is used for onboarding, performance management, talent management, employee sentiment analysis, recruitment, employee churn, learning and development, as well as compensation.

DBS Bank Uses JIM to Recruit New Employees

For many organizations, recruiting can take a significant amount of time and resources. Getting the right candidate into the right role is paramount, as poor choices can be costly and detrimental for both the new employee and the employer. DBS Bank in Singapore created JIM—the Job Intelligence Maestro application—to accelerate the recruiting process. Continually operating in real-time, JIM reviews resumes, collects responses to screening questions, answers candidate questions, and conducts profile assessments—saving about 40 human-hours per month.[35] DBS has also developed an employee-attrition model that uses data like training, compensation, and leave patterns to predict whether or not an associate will quit the organization.[36]

Service and Support

If customer service is done well, 77% of customers will be more loyal and 75% will spend more. But if it's done poorly, half will switch to other companies after just one bad experience.[37] In a service and support organization, AI can be used for call center optimization, predictive maintenance, sentiment analysis, emotion detection, next-best offer, call routing, service ticket categorization, and much more.

Amazon Uses AI to Improve Customer Service[38]

As one of the largest online retailers in the world, Amazon is responsible for 40% of online spending in the United States.[39] One of its primary goals is to be a world-class service business. Amazon is using AI to forecast on-time deliveries in a global supply system that has 400 million products forecasted every day. It has over 300 fulfillment centers, 200,000 robots, 19,000 trailers, and 30,000 delivery vans. On Prime day, 3,000 orders are received per minute. To help maximize success, predictive shipping is used to put the right items in the right place even before the customer clicks the "Buy" button. In addition to supply chain automation, AI is used to personalize music and video recommendations with a service called StyleSnap that matches uses images to help customers find products. Computer vision and other technologies are used to eliminate checkout lines in stores.

Another example is **Nestle** has developing a "Cookie Coach" named Ruth to help you bake that perfect cookie.[40] Nestle states that 70% of the calls to its customer service hotline were related to questions about the iconic recipe.

AI Across Industries

In addition to organizations using AI across every aspect of business, AI is also used across every industry. In this next section, we'll go over examples across banking and finance, energy and utilities, insurance, government and public sector, healthcare, life sciences, manufacturing, retail, telecom, and transportation and logistics.

Banking and Finance

For banking and finance, AI is used to hyper-personalize end-to-end customer experiences. It is being used to engage customers more thoroughly and effectively and also to automate processes such as fraud detection, churn prediction and prevention, payment processing, cash reconciliation, underwriting, and claims management. Additional use cases include embezzlement and expense fraud, pricing, asset evaluation, forecasting, bad debt management, and anti-money laundering.

Bank of America's Chatbot "Erica" Surpasses 100 million Interactions

As the COVID-19 pandemic continues to disrupt society and our "normal" way of life, people are increasingly turning toward online banking apps. In fact, 50% of consumers interacted with banking apps in 2020 (up from 32% in the previous year) and 72% of banks expect interactions through human chat will increase in the next couple of years.[41] Bank of America launched a chatbot named "Erica" in 2018. In the first quarter of 2021, Erica had over 19.5 million clients, 105.6 million interactions, has answered over 250 million questions. And the best part is Erica can respond to more than a million unique financial questions.[42]

Energy and Utilities

Energy and utility companies use AI for a wide variety of use cases. Common examples include predictive machine maintenance, field equipment sensor analytics, workforce support, and safety. Furthermore, companies are using computer vision and ML in dangerous working conditions as well as for utility service outages and predictive insights.

Xcel Energy Uses AI to Reliably Predict Renewable Energy

In the energy sector, being able to reliably predict power available to the market is a key factor in a company's profitability. Renewables like wind, although better for the environment, pose special challenges. Wind is variable and notoriously difficult to predict. Essentially, companies make more money if they can sell their energy in advance rather than in real time. DeepMind (an AI company owned by Google) combines weather and power data for 700 megawatts of energy sourced in the United States. This data is used to better predict how windy it will be the next day and has resulted in a 20% increase in revenue for wind farms.[43] One large Midwestern company, Xcel Energy, has partnered with the National Center for Atmospheric Research to provide more accurate wind forecasts. The margin of error of forecasts has been reduced by 40%, resulting in a $60M reduction of costs for end customers and millions of tons of carbon emissions saved annually due to less reliance on coal and gas.[44]

Insurance

In the insurance industry, AI is used across product development, marketing and sales, policy administration, as well as claims processing. Key use cases include support and recommendations for insurance agents, marketing, automated underwriting, fraud detection, claims processing, claims estimation, churn, and customer service.

GEICO Uses AI to Automate Auto Insurance Claims

The United States' second largest auto insurer, GEICO uses AI to automate the process for automobile insurance claims.[45] Historically, if someone had to file an insurance claim, the policyholder would make an appointment with an insurance adjuster or visit a repair shop. This could take days to complete, causing quite a bit of frustration for the policy holder. In partnership with the AI-firm Tractable, a mechanic can now use a smartphone or similar device to forward pictures of the damage. The AI then either auto approves the claim or sends it to a human adjuster to refine the claim. For large insurers with millions of claims per year, a traditional approach with a human reviewer could take 30 minutes to process each claim. With the Tractable AI technology, it is estimated that 70% of claims can be automated.[46] Unlike other insurers, GEICO is using the AI to verify submitted claims on the back end rather than providing original estimates.

By using AI, insurance companies are improving customer satisfaction, operational efficiency, while ensuring consistency and accuracy and reducing processing time.

Government and Public Sector

AI is used across a variety of government and public sector domains. Use cases span environmental monitoring and protection, law enforcement and public safety, utilities and infrastructure, back-office operations, transportation, and human services. Examples include weather and scenario planning for environmental changes and disasters, asset management (i.e., waste bins, parking meters, fire hydrants, vehicle fleets, etc.), predictive policing and crime hot-spotting, HR benefits automation, food distribution, and more. There are also numerous AI applications associated with national defense that is beyond the scope of this book.

NYC Automates Expected Billing Values and Payments

New York City's (NYC) Department of Citywide Administrative Services (DCAS) has a team responsible for paying the city's utilities—including electricity, gas, and steam bills. The division is also responsible for budgeting, so understanding and monitoring what's being spent is important. But some charges can be irregular and the billing structure is quite complex. With over 15,000 monthly bills, the volume is simply too much for manual review. The DCAS team built a predictive ML model that included millions of previous bills, weather data, and facility information (e.g., year built, square footage, and usage types). The ML models are quite accurate and can frequently predict the amount of an expected bill (within cents). However, when the prediction is off by more than a specific percentage, it is sent to a human for review. The system has saved millions of dollars, including more than $4.5M in refunds in 2020 and 2021 from over 100 billing anomalies.[47]

This is a great example of back-office automation. Similarly, the US Department of Health and Human Services processes over 70,000 applications per month using AI for back-office automation.[48]

Healthcare

In the healthcare industry, AI is used by both payers and providers.

For payers, applications span personalized experiences and customer engagement, population health management, and alignment with providers, partners, purchasers, and regulators. Examples include support for chronic conditions and diseases, payment claims processing, home health monitoring, and claims support. There is tremendous opportunity to automate many of the administrative tasks in the healthcare industry.

For providers, applications span disease prevention and management of diagnosis, treatment, recovery, and monitoring. Examples include help with disease diagnoses, managing reproductive needs, automatically detecting anomalies in radiology and pathology images, etc. It is also used for virtual health assistance, algorithmic medicine, clinical automation, precision medicine, and clinical documentation support. As uses grow, AI will create smarter hospitals and better treatment options for patients.

Using AI to Detect Lung Cancer

Lung cancer is one of the deadliest in the world. In 2021, the United States attributed over 131,000 fatalities to it, making it one of the leading causes of death.[49,50] If not detected early, 75% will die within five years of diagnosis—so the earlier it is detected, the better.[51] Traditionally, radiologists have to manually review CT scans. However, humans may overlook small anomalies in a scan. There are computer technologies that a human has to guide but many benign tumors are flagged. AI systems were given historical images to figure out how to spot tumors. One system "correctly identified the early stages of lung cancer 94% of the time, outperforming a panel of six veteran radiologists" that typical have an accuracy rate of 65%.[52]

The benefits of AI in healthcare include improved member health status, medical costs management, better customer experiences, increases in revenue, and operational cost reductions.

For providers, benefits include financial wellness, improved health, improved patient engagement, and lower costs.

Life Sciences

In the life sciences, AI is used in the manufacturing process, clinical trials, marketing, and patient engagement. Examples include integrated clinical trial data from multiple source systems and automatically populating data fields. For manufacturing, it's used to maximize factory yield and optimize performance, and AI is used for simulations to assess various parameters as well. Additionally, it is used for the patient experience, marketing, monitoring for adverse reactions, and risk and compliance. It's also used to analyze the notes of sales reps to ensure adherence to regulations.

Biotech Company Evotec Uses AI to Accelerate Cancer Drug Development

Traditionally, the drug discovery process can take up to five years to identify drug candidates. The German biotech company Evotec partnered with the UK-based AI company Exscientia that specializes in AI-related drug discovery. The joint system was able to analyze and compare "various properties of millions of small molecules, looking for 10 or 20 to synthesize, test and optimize in lab experiments before selecting the eventual drug candidate for clinical trials."[53] The system was able to discover a new candidate within eight months!

Benefits include reduced costs, increased revenue, improved customer experience, and innovation.

Manufacturing

In the manufacturing industry, AI is used across R&D, product design, and the manufacturing process. Important use cases include predictive maintenance, automatic defect classification, process optimization, smart sampling, energy management, etc.

BMW Group Uses AI for Paint Quality

BMW Group manufactures BMW, Mini, and Rolls-Royce vehicles. With over 120,000 employees (2020), it operates 31 different production facilities across 15 countries; maintaining high-quality standards is paramount to its success.[54] BMW has been using AI and computer vision since 2018.[55] For example, any dust that may be present in the air when painting automobiles is a risk. BMW uses AI to help predict when dust levels are increasing (e.g., during dry periods) and the need to perform automatic surface inspections (ASIs). "The company states that data from sensors and surface inspections enables over 160 features relating to the car body to be monitored and the quality of the paint application can be predicted very accurately."[56] With this technology, increased levels of poor paint quality are detected and the production line can be stopped to make process improvements in real time.

Benefits of using AI in manufacturing include reduced costs, improved operational efficiency, greater yield, quality improvement, and accelerated time to market.

For example, in the semiconductor industry, AI is used across the end-to-end value chain.[57]

Retail

In retail, AI is used across the entire value chain—from when the consumer is searching for products to sales and post-purchase activities. Examples include assortment planning and optimization, price setting, promotions, mark-down optimization, fraud detection, customer-demand prediction, determining next-best actions, planning, forecasting, and marketing.

Stitch Fix Personalizes Fashion and Clothing Recommendations

Founded in 2011, Stitch Fix is one of the world's fastest growing retailers. Essentially, customers sign up for the Stitch Fix service and answer a few "style" questions when setting up their profile. The company then mails clients a "Fix." This is a personalized box of clothing that matches their preference. Stitch Fix uses a combination of stylists (humans) and algorithms to personalize the boxes, employing approximately 3,700 stylists and 140 data scientists.[58,59] If customers want the box, they keep it. If not, they return it free of charge. As of October 30, 2021, the company had $2.2B in revenue and 4.2 million active clients. Figure 4.1 illustrates Data Collected by Stitch Fix.[60] Benefits include reduced costs and increase revenue.

Figure 4.1 Stitch Fix Data

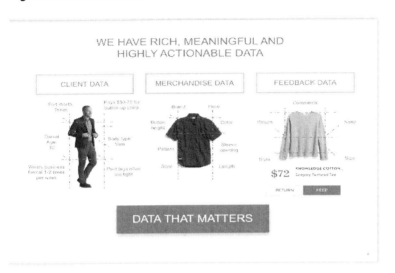

Another example is **Facebook**, which has created technology to generate recipes directly from food images taken with smartphones. **Samsung** can also generate recipes by analyzing the food that in your fridge.[61,62]

Telecom

AI is used across a variety of domains in the telecommunications and networking sector. It is used for planning, monitoring, network diagnostics, and optimization. Contact center automation uses NLP (natural language processing) and ML (machine learning) to improve the customer experience. Telecom providers use AI to automate customer engagement and communication, detect fake media content, predict customer behaviors and next-best action, and increase personalization.

Verizon Uses AI for 5G Cell Tower Placement

Compared to 4G networks, 5G can increase Internet speeds by a factor of 100. However, since 5G uses a higher frequency, it has a shorter range. Thus, providers need to install more 5G transmitters than with 4G. Some estimates predict the rollout will cost an estimated $750B.[63] From a business perspective, it takes significant investment to install all these transmitters, so it makes sense to maximize coverage with the least number of them. Verizon uses AI to optimize tower locations. Using computer vision, "The models, designed by in-house data scientists and other employees, factor in a number of variables that can alter the strength of 5G signals, like buildings, bridges, terrain, the position of the transmitter, as well as other transmitters nearby."[64]

Benefits include cost efficiency, quality, and customer experience.

Other ML use cases in the telecom sector are illustrated in Table 4.1.[65]

Table 4.1: Machine Learning Use Cases in Telecom

System Monitoring	Managed Services	Intelligent Networks
Anomaly Detection	Ticket Classification	Self-Healing

System Monitoring	Managed Services	Intelligent Networks
Root Cause Identification	Churn Prediction	Dynamic Optimization
Predictive Maintenance	SLA Assurance	Automated Network Design

Transportation and Logistics

AI is used quite extensively in the transportation and logistics domain. It is used for planning, fleet management, transport, and improved customer experience. Use cases include estimated time arrivals (ETA), asset performance, optimization, scheduling, etc. Additionally, it's used for fleet network optimization, and real-time decision-making regarding traffic, weather, road conditions, etc.

FedEx Provides Real-Time Package Analytics and Robotic Delivery

The logistics juggernaut FedEx connects more than 99% of the world's gross domestic product across 220 countries and territories, delivering more than 6.6 million packages a day.[66,67] For customers with time-sensitive supply chain needs—for items like pharmaceuticals, food, medical supplies, and perishables—having real-time understanding of supply chain disruptions is critical. FedEx has integrated AI and ML into its tracking systems to provide near-real-time visibility on goods in transit. Additionally, this service—dubbed FedEx Surround—provides customers with notifications on global shipping conditions that could disrupt package-delivery dates—things like natural disasters.[68] Also, FedEx is experimenting with same-day delivery with autonomous bots (Roxo, the FedEx SameDay Bot) as well as drone delivery with Wing.[69]

Benefits include efficiency gains, cost reductions, and better service, revenues, and safety.

Summary

In this chapter, we looked at examples of AI's use across industries and lines of business functions, as well as benefits associated with each. The primary goal was to provide some inspiration on the art of what is possible for your organization. In many of these examples, the businesses used a variety of data sources (transactional, image, geospatial, behavioral, and genetic) and techniques. A myriad of ML methods were used, including NLP, computer vision, chatbots, and automation technologies like RPA.

Chapter 4 References

1   "Gartner Finance Research Shows Bad Debt Increased 26% in 2020." Gartner. July 7, 2021. https://www.gartner.com/en/newsroom/press-releases/2021-07-07-gartner-finance-research-shows-bad-debt-increased-26-percent-in-2020.

2   Duffy, Nigel, and Karsten Fuser. "Six Ways the CFO Can Use Artificial Intelligence, Today." EY. September 19, 2019. https://www.ey.com/en_us/ai/six-ways-the-cfo-can-use-artificial-intelligence-today.

3   Duffy, Nigel (Karsten Füser, ed.). "Five Ways CFOs Can Use AI: Today." CFO. July 3, 2019. https://www.cfo.com/analytics/2019/07/five-ways-cfos-can-use-ai-today/.

4   Maurer, Mark. "Airbus Harnessing AI in Bid to Save Millions on Finance Tasks." Wall Street Journal. August 19, 2019. https://www.wsj.com/articles/airbus-harnessing-ai-in-bid-to-save-millions-on-finance-tasks-11566207002.

5   "Equinix: Opening Your Eyes to the Power of OCR and RPA." BrightTALK. April 19, 2019. https://www.brighttalk.com/webcast/17260/351787.

6   "How a Company Used AI to Expedite ASC 842 Compliance." Financial Executives International. June 24, 2019. https://www.financialexecutives.org/FEI-Daily/June-2019/How-a-Company-Used-AI-to-Expedite-ASC-842-Complian.aspx.

7   "Product Information." PepsiCo. 2021. https://www.pepsico.com/brands/product-information.

8   "About the Company." PepsiCo. 2021. https://www.pepsico.com/about/about-the-company.

9   Ransbotham, Sam (Shervin Khodabandeh, ed.). "No Need for AI Unicorns: PepsiCo's Colin Lenaghan." MIT Sloan Management Review. June 8, 2021. https://sloanreview.mit.edu/audio/no-need-for-ai-unicorns-pepsicos-colin-lenaghan/.

10 Tully, Shawn. "Fortune 500 Companies Are Raising Prices: And Consumers Don't Seem to Care." Fortune. October 12, 2021. https://fortune.com/2021/10/12/fortune-500-companies-are-raising-prices-and-consumers-dont-seem-to-care/.

11 Beckett, Emma Liem. "Starbucks' Digital Success Partially Driven by AI Engine, CEO Kevin Johnson Says." Restaurant Dive. April 28, 2021. https://www.restaurantdive.com/news/starbucks-digital-success-partially-driven-by-ai-engine-ceo-kevin-johnson/599182/.

12 Ryan, Tom. "Will Tech Acquisitions Enable Nike to Drive Personalization at Scale?" RetailWire. March 22, 2021. https://www.retailwire.com/discussion/will-tech-acquisitions-enable-nike-to-drive-personalization-at-scale/.

13 Ives, Nat. "JPMorgan Chase Taps AI to Make Marketing Messages More Powerful." Wall Street Journal. July 30, 2019. https://www.wsj.com/articles/jpmorgan-chase-taps-ai-to-make-marketing-messages-more-powerful-11564482606.

14 "AI in Creativity Removes the Blindspot in Marketing." Persado. May 17, 2021. https://www.persado.com/articles/ai-in-creativity-removes-the-blindspot-in-marketing/.

15 May, Michael. "Next Level AI: Powered by Knowledge Graphs and Data Thinking Siemens China Innovation Day." Siemens. May 15, 2019. https://assets.new.siemens.com/siemens/assets/public.1559011182.cb8f9288-6f4a-4568-b8fe-7a1c03deef5b.15-22-may-en-ai-presentation-sid-2019-dr--michael-may-en-final-0.pdf.

16 Columbus, Louis. "10 Ways AI Is Improving New Product Development." Forbes. July 9, 2020. https://www.forbes.com/sites/louiscolumbus/2020/07/09/10-ways-ai-is-improving-new-product-development/?sh=22158bea5d3c.

17 "Product Design Gets an AI Makeover." MIT Technology Review. May 10, 2021. https://www.technologyreview.com/2021/05/10/1024531/product-design-gets-an-ai-makeover/.

18 "Product Design Gets an AI Makeover with Artificial Intelligence, Simulation Software Makes Engineers' Jobs Easier, Improves Production Processes, and Spurs Innovation." MIT Technology Review Insights. n.d. Accessed December 2, 2021. https://wp.technologyreview.com/wp-content/uploads/2021/05/Product-design-gets-an-AI-makeover.pdf.

19 Ransbotham, Sam, and Shervin Khodabandeh. "AI and the COVID-19 Vaccine: Moderna's Dave Johnson." MIT Sloan Management Review. July 13, 2021. https://sloanreview.

mit.edu/audio/ai-and-the-covid-19-vaccine-modernas-dave-johnson/.

20 Chiappetta, Marco. "Chips Designed by AI Are the Future of Semiconductor Evolution beyond Moore's Law." Forbes. May 25, 2021. https://www.forbes.com/sites/marcochiappetta/2021/05/25/chips-designed-by-ai-are-the-future-of-semiconductor-evolution-beyond-moores-law/?sh=107b96a3430f.

21 Castellanos, Sara. "Tyson Takes Computer Vision to the Chicken Plant." Wall Street Journal. February 10, 2020. https://www.wsj.com/articles/tyson-takes-computer-vision-to-the-chicken-plant-11581330602.

22 Lagunas, Jamie, and John Matchette. "Supply Chain Analytics and AI in Driving Relevance, Resilience and Responsibility." Accenture. September 22, 2021. https://www.accenture.com/cr-en/insights/artificial-intelligence/supply-chain-analytics-ai.

23 Schroeder, Eric. "Nestle Debuts Ruth, the 'Cookie Coach.'" Baking Business. March 9, 2021. https://www.bakingbusiness.com/articles/53177-nestle-debuts-ruth-the-cookie-coach.

24 Lu, Gwendolyn. "How Procter & Gamble Is Leveraging AI to Constructively Disrupt Supply Chain and Retail Execution." VentureBeat. July 12, 2021. https://venturebeat.com/2021/07/12/how-procter-gamble-is-leveraging-ai-to-constructively-disrupt-supply-chain-and-retail-execution.

25 "For Procter & Gamble, Data Is at the Heart of Digital Transformation." Microsoft Customers Stories. August 17, 2021. https://customers.microsoft.com/en-us/story/1402016901008352804-procter-and-gamble-consumer-goods-azure.

26 Mefford, Doug. "How AI Is Transforming Global Supply Chains." SupplyChainBrain. December 8, 2020. https://www.supplychainbrain.com/blogs/1-think-tank/post/32330-how-ai-is-transforming-global-supply-chains.

27 Dignan, Larry. "How Technology and Data Make Walmart Shine amid Supply Chain Issues, Inflation." ZDNet. November 16, 2016. https://www.zdnet.com/article/how-technology-and-data-make-walmart-shine-amid-supply-chain-issues-inflation/.

28 "DHL Express Deploys AI-Powered Sorting Robot." DHL. September 7, 2021. https://www.dhl.com/cn-en/home/press/press-archive/2021/dhl-express-deploys-ai-powered-sorting-robot.html.

29 Leggett, David. 2021. "How Audi Is Using AI as a Supply Chain Risk Radar." Just Auto. June 18, 2021. https://www.just-auto.com/features/how-audi-is-using-ai-as-a-supply-chain-risk-radar/.

30 "Definition of AIOps (Artificial Intelligence for IT Operations): Gartner Information Technology Glossary." Gartner. n.d. Accessed December 2, 2021. https://www.gartner.com/en/information-technology/glossary/aiops-artificial-intelligence-operations.

31 Reddy, Rakesh. "6 Major AI Use Cases in IT Operations." Acuvate. December 14, 2020. https://acuvate.com/blog/ai-use-cases-in-it-operations/.

32 Ashley, John. "American Express Adopts NVIDIA AI to Help Prevent Fraud and Foil Cybercrime." NVIDIA Blog. October 5, 2020. https://blogs.nvidia.com/blog/2020/10/05/american-express-nvidia-ai/.

33 West, Darrell M. "Using AI and Machine Learning to Reduce Government Fraud." Brookings. September 10, 2021. https://www.brookings.edu/research/using-ai-and-machine-learning-to-reduce-government-fraud/.

34 Zheng, Huaixiu. "COTA: Improving Uber Customer Care with NLP & Machine Learning." Uber Engineering. January 3, 2018. https://eng.uber.com/cota/.

35 "Creating Jim, SEA's First Recruitment Chatbot." DBS Innovates. November 1, 2018. https://www.dbs.com/

innovation/dbs-innovates/creating-jim-southeast-asias-first-recruitment-chatbot.html.

36 Bean, Randy, and Thomas H. Davenport. "Portrait of an AI Leader: Piyush Gupta of DBS Bank." MIT Sloan Management Review. August 31, 2021. https://sloanreview.mit.edu/article/portrait-of-an-ai-leader-piyush-gupta-of-dbs-bank/.

37 Gupta, Courtney. "Customer Service Definition: Skills, Types, Roles & Rules." Zendesk. May 26, 2021. https://www.zendesk.com/blog/customer-service-skills/.

38 "AWS Re: Invent 2020; Amazon.com's Use of AI/ML to Enhance the Customer Experience [video]." YouTube. March 5, 2021. https://youtu.be/jADP7RmqW2g.

39 Ovide, Shira. "How Big Is Amazon, Really?" New York Times. March 30, 2021. https://www.nytimes.com/2021/03/30/technology/amazon-market-size.html.

40 Schroeder, Eric. "Nestle Debuts Ruth, the 'Cookie Coach.'" Baking Business. March 9, 2021. https://www.bakingbusiness.com/articles/53177-nestle-debuts-ruth-the-cookie-coach.

41 Kirschfink, Adrien, Bruce Holley, Edwin Van de Ouderaa, and Anne Bertelsen. "Banking on Empathy Engaging with Customers in a More Human Way." Accenture. 2021. https://bankingblog.accenture.com/wp-content/uploads/2021/04/Banking-On-Empathy-Accenture.pdf.

42 Schwartz, Eric. "Bank of America's Virtual Assistant Erica Explodes in Popularity." Voicebot.ai. April 21, 2021. https://voicebot.ai/2021/04/21/bank-of-americas-virtual-assistant-erica-explodes-in-popularity/.

43 McMahon, Jeff. "Thanks to Renewables and Machine Learning, Google Now Forecasts the Wind." Forbes. May 31, 2020. https://www.forbes.com/sites/jeffmcmahon/2020/05/31/thanks-to-renewables-and-machine-learning-google-now-forecasts-the-wind/?sh=4a369e9e1865.

44 TOMB2020. "Xcel Energy: Utilizing Machine Learning to Efficiently and Reliably Incorporate Renewable Energy into the U.S. Energy Grid." Technology and Operations Management. November 13, 2018. https://digital.hbs.edu/platform-rctom/submission/xcel-energy-utilizing-machine-learning-to-efficiently-and-reliably-incorporate-renewable-energy-into-the-u-s-energy-grid/.

45 Scism, Leslie, and Geoffrey Rogow. "Geico to Use Artificial Intelligence to Speed up Car Repairs." Wall Street Journal. May 25, 2021. https://www.wsj.com/articles/geico-to-use-artificial-intelligence-to-speed-up-car-repairs-11621944000.

46 Huetter, John. "GEICO to Use Tractable AI Review to Double-Check Estimates." Repairer Driven News. May 27, 2021. https://www.repairerdrivennews.com/2021/05/27/geico-to-use-tractable-ai-to-double-check-estimates/.

47 "Mayor's Office of the Chief Technology Officer." NYC Mayor's Office of the Chief Technology Officer. October 13, 2021. https://www1.nyc.gov/assets/cto/downloads/ai-strategy/nyc_ai_strategy.pdf.

48 "The AI Dossier." Deloitte. 2021. https://www2.deloitte.com/content/dam/Deloitte/us/Documents/deloitte-analytics/us-ai-institute-ai-dossier-full-report.pdf.

49 National Cancer Institute. "Cancer of the Lung and Bronchus: Cancer Stat Facts." SEER. 2018. https://seer.cancer.gov/statfacts/html/lungb.html.

50 Siwicki, Bill. "AI Deployments Accelerating across an Array of Complex Use Cases." Healthcare IT News. June 22, 2021. https://www.healthcareitnews.com/news/ai-deployments-accelerating-across-array-complex-use-cases.

51 Svoboda, Elizabeth. "Artificial Intelligence Is Improving the Detection of Lung Cancer." Nature 587, no. 7834 (2020): S20–22. https://doi.org/10.1038/d41586-020-03157-9.

52 Ibid.

53 Savage, Neil. "Tapping into the Drug Discovery Potential of AI." Biopharma Dealmakers. May 27, 2021. https://doi.org/10.1038/d43747-021-00045-7.

54 "Company." BMW Group. 2017. https://www.bmwgroup.com/en/company.html.

55 "AI-Based Quality Control for Every Employee." Metrology and Quality News. September 30, 2021. https://metrology.news/ai-based-quality-control-for-every-employee/.

56 Farish, Mike. "AI Data Analytics for the Paintshop." Automotive Manufacturing Solutions. December 17, 2021. https://www.automotivemanufacturingsolutions.com/bmw/ai-data-analytics-for-the-paintshop/42584.article.

57 Göke, Sebastian, Kevin Staight, and Rutger Vrijen. "Scaling AI in the Sector That Enables It: Lessons for Semiconductor-Device Makers." McKinsey. 2021. https://www.mckinsey.com/~/media/mckinsey/industries/semiconductors/our%20insights/scaling%20ai%20in%20the%20sector%20that%20enables%20it%20lessons%20for%20semiconductor%20device%20makers/scaling-ai-in-the-sector-that-enables-it.pdf.

58 Davenport, Tom. "The Future of Work Now: AI-Assisted Clothing Stylists at Stitch Fix." Forbes. March 12, 2021. https://www.forbes.com/sites/tomdavenport/2021/03/12/the-future-of-work-now-ai-assisted-clothing-stylists-at-stitch-fix/?sh=1b9040d73590.

59 "Stitch Fix Investor Presentation." Stitch Fix. December 7, 2021. https://investors.stitchfix.com/static-files/01c3262e-8900-44df-a960-e8a262b587e3.

60 "Stitch Fix Investor Presentation." Stitch Fix. December 7, 2021. https://investors.stitchfix.com/static-files/01c3262e-8900-44df-a960-e8a262b587e3.

61 Romero, Adriana, Michal Drozdzal, and Julia Peter. "Using AI to Generate Recipes from Food Images." Meta AI. n.d. Accessed January 29, 2022. https://ai.facebook.com/blog/inverse-cooking/.

62 "New Tech Suggests Recipes Based on the Food Already in Your Fridge." ABC News. July 8, 2020. https://abcnews.go.com/Technology/tech-suggests-recipies-based-food-fridge/story?id=68152071.

63 McCartney, Robert. "Perspective: The Ugly Side of 5G; New Cell Towers Spoil the Scenery and Crowd People's Homes." Washington Post. July 12, 2021. https://www.washingtonpost.com/local/5g-towers-dewey-beach/2021/07/11/455e3866-e0f4-11eb-9f54-7eee10b5fcd2_story.html.

64 Castellanos, Sara. "Tyson Takes Computer Vision to the Chicken Plant." Wall Street Journal. February 10, 2020. https://www.wsj.com/articles/tyson-takes-computer-vision-to-the-chicken-plant-11581330602.

65 Butakov, Nikita, Loren Jan Wilson, Wenting Sun, and Angel Barranco. "Exploring Machine Learning Use Cases in Telecom." Ericsson. May 26, 2021. https://www.ericsson.com/en/blog/2021/5/machine-learning-use-cases-in-telecom.

66 "FedEx and Microsoft Join Forces to Transform Commerce." FedEx Newsroom. May 18, 2020. https://newsroom.fedex.com/newsroom/fedex-surround/.

67 "FedEx Express: Total Average Daily Packages 2020." Statista. n.d. Accessed December 30, 2021. https://www.statista.com/statistics/878354/fedex-express-total-average-daily-packages/.

68 Gordon, Cindy. "Advancing AI Revenue Growth and Operations Insights in the Transportation and Logistics Industry." Forbes. October 31, 2021. https://www.forbes.com/sites/cindygordon/2021/10/31/advancing-ai-revenue-growth-insights-in-the-transportation-and-logistics-industryindustry-series-blog-4/?sh=648cb7464457.

69 "Technology and Innovation." FedEx. 2019. https://www.fedex.com/en-us/about/policy/technology-innovation.html.

Chapter 5

Why Is AI Used?

In Chapter 4, we examined how AI is used across line of business functions and various industries and shared a wide variety of case studies and other use cases for each of the domain areas. In this chapter, we'll look at why AI is used in organizations. Before emphasizing all the financial improvements that result from AI, we need to make sure we are clear on business processes and digital decisions.

Digital Decisions

Every second of every day, organizations are continually making decisions. When informed by data and analytics, we can classify them as "digital decisions." In some cases, these decisions are automated; in others, a human is in the loop. Either way, these are digital decisions. When data and analytics are used to make a decision, we can consider it a flow as illustrated in Figure 5.1.

Figure 5.1: Digital Decision Process Flow

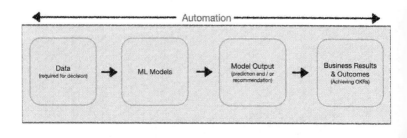

Types of Decisions

On any given day, an organization may make millions of decisions. Some are tiny and some more impactful. These can run the gamut from "Should we grant this individual credit for a mortgage?" to "Does this medical image show a potential anomaly?" In general, decisions can be classified into three types: strategic, tactical, and operational.

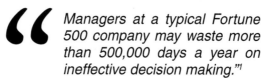 *Managers at a typical Fortune 500 company may waste more than 500,000 days a year on ineffective decision making."[1]*

Strategic Decisions

On the other hand, organizations generally make only a few strategic decisions every year. These typically involve a board of directors and the executive leadership team. For the most part, each is unique to the specific decision, but often with far-reaching impacts on the organization.

Strategic decisions include:

- Should we build a banking branch?
- Should we enter or exit a specific market?
- Do we want to acquire this company?

Strategic decisions are complex, unique, and in many instances, not repeatable. There are different decision-making frameworks that help people think through critical issues in a systematic and structured way, but in the end ingenuity, creative problem-solving, and risk assessments are required to make effective decisions.

Tactical Decisions

Tactical decisions define the methods, policies, products, services, and procedures used to support the organization's strategic decisions. There are comparatively many more tactical decisions made in an organization.

Examples include:

- What is an acceptable level of insurance risk?
- What are the specific levels of inventory that we would like to carry?
- What staffing levels do we to set for our departments?

Operational Decisions

Once a set of strategic and tactical decisions have been made, operational decisions support these processes. These are the most prolific types of decisions that exist in an organization.

Examples include:

- Is this part we manufactured potentially defective?
- Is this particular transaction fraudulent?
- What is the next-best offer we should make to a prospective customer?

Operational decisions are known, structured, and repeatable. There are often thousands upon thousands of them occurring in your business every day. These are typically the kinds of decisions organizations look to automate with AI.

Human vs. Automated Decisions

For organizations that have not yet automated digital decisions, there is usually a human still in the loop. If we apply AI to make decisions, does a human still need to be involved? Will AI take our jobs? Fortunately, it's not an all-or-nothing approach. An industry analyst firm IDC has developed a five-level framework of the decision types:[2]

1. Human Lead
2. Human Lead, Machine Supported
3. Machine Lead, Human Supported
4. Machine Lead, Human Governed
5. Machine Controlled

Table 5.1 below, adapted from IDC, further breaks down these categories in terms of who produces the insights, who decides (and how they do so), and who acts based on the decision.

Table 5.1: Human and Machines Decision Types

	Human-led	Human-led, machine-supported	Machine-led, human-supported	Machine-led, human-governed	Machine-controlled
Who produces insights?	Human analyzes and produces insights using limited tools.	Human analyzes and produces insights based on multiple tools.	Machine analyzes and produces insights, then human reviews.	Machine analyzes and produces insights without human review.	Machine analyzes and controls.
Who decides and how?	Human decides based on experience and heuristics.	Human decides based on machine recommendations.	Human decides based on recommendations and simulations.	Machine decides based on heuristics and human governance framework.	Machine decides.

	Human-led	Human-led, machine-supported	Machine-led, human-supported	Machine-led, human-governed	Machine-controlled
Who acts based on decisions?	Human acts or executes.	Human acts or executes.	Human acts or executes with machine oversight and automation.	Machine acts or executes with machine automation and human oversight.	Machine acts or executes.

Why Analytics and Automation?

The Business Value of Insights

In your organization, all data results from business events. Once one occurs, the information value associated with the data begins to decay. The following steps typically occur when a business event occurs:[3]

Business Event → Data Stored → Information Delivered → Action Taken

To maximize the value you receive from that data, you need to analyze it as fast as possible.

The information value decays over time as illustrated by Figure 5.1, which compares the value of a decision versus time.

Figure 5.1: Information Value of Insights

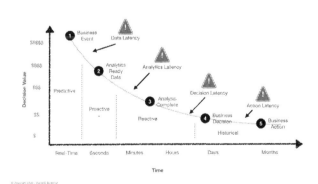

As you can see from the diagram, latency can occur at every step of the process. In this example, we see data, analytics, decision, and action latency.

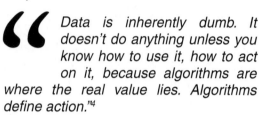

> *Data is inherently dumb. It doesn't do anything unless you know how to use it, how to act on it, because algorithms are where the real value lies. Algorithms define action."[4]*
>
> —*Gartner*

AI can be used to automate processes and shorten the event-to-action cycle. The faster we can make decisions, the more value we receive, as illustrated in Figure 5.2.

Figure 5.2: Maximizing the Value of Data by Shortening Event to Action

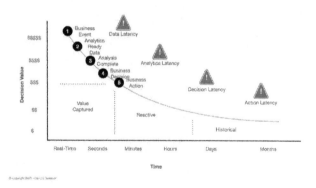

The Value of Analytics and Automation

Now that we understand the types of decisions that can be made and the information value of insights, what value does analytics and automation bring to an organization? Research shows that companies that use analytics and AI outperform those that do not. There is a common analytics maturity assessment that companies can take to understand where they rate on a maturity scale. Most survey instruments use a five-point scale. One is the least "analytically mature" while five is the most. On a five-point scale, with five being the most analytically mature when comparing companies, you will see that companies with higher analytic maturity outperform those with a lower maturity score. This is seen across all financial dimensions, including revenue, operating income, and return on investment (ROI). This is illustrated in Figure 5.3.[5]

Figure 5.3: Five-Year Financial Performance Comparison By AI Maturity

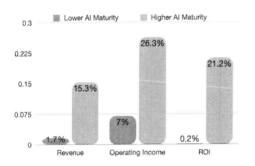

Every business function can benefit from AI technology. Using the same data as above, revenue increases occurred most often in marketing and sales, with 40% of respondents reporting 5% gains and 30% of respondents with 6%–10% gains. Cost decreases occurred most often in manufacturing, with 37% of respondents reporting decreases of over 10%.[6]

Why Is AI Used?

Remember the quiz in <u>Chapter 1</u>? Well, as promised, <u>Figure 5.4</u> provides an overview of the core practices that top-performing organizations use to scale AI.

Figure 5.4: Core Practices to Scale AI

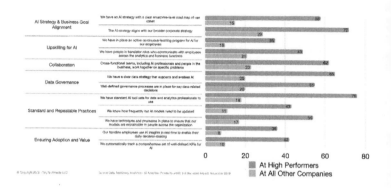

This data was collected from a McKinsey survey in which respondents were asked to state whether their organization had any of these practices.[7] As you can see from the chart, 58% of respondents in "High Performing" companies had an AI strategy with a clear enterprise-level roadmap of use cases compared to 15% at other companies. That's a 3.9X difference in performance! High-performing companies used a variety of strategies that allowed them to scale AI across the organization. We also see that AI tool sets (4.2X difference), AI mapped to KPIs (4.2X), model monitoring/ops (3.9X), continuous learning programs (3.5X difference), a clear data strategy (3.3X difference), and adoption by frontline employees (4.5X) are the key differentiators.

Summary

In this chapter, we discussed the types of decisions that organizations make and emphasized that AI is most frequently applied to operational decisions since those are standardized and repeatable. By shortening the event to an insight cycle, organizations can realize significant benefits across all business functions. We also examined the core principles needed to scale AI across an organization.

Chapter 5 References

1   Smet, Aaron De, Gregor Jost, and Leigh Weiss. "Three Keys to Better Decision Making." McKinsey. May 1, 2019. https://www.mckinsey.com/business-functions/people-and-organizational-performance/our-insights/three-keys-to-faster-better-decisions.

2   Vesset, Dan. "Introducing IDC's AI-Based Automation Evolution Framework." IDC Blog. January 9, 2019. https://blogs.idc.com/2019/01/09/idcs-ai-based-automation-evolution-framework-a-new-way-to-think-about-ai-automation/.

3   Rozsnyai, Szabolcs, Josef Schiefer, and Heinz Roth. "SARI-SQL: Event Query Language for Event Analysis." 2009 IEEE Conference on Commerce and Enterprise Computing (pp. 24–32). Washington, DC: IEEE Computer Society, 2009. https://doi.org/10.1109/cec.2009.14.

4   Chanthadavong, Aimee. "Big Data Is Useless without Algorithms, Gartner Says." ZDNet. October 26, 2015. https://www.zdnet.com/article/big-data-is-useless-without-algorithms-gartner-says/.

5   Phillips, Jack, and David Alles. "Analytics Maturity & Company Performance/ROI." International Institute for

Analytics. July 14, 2020. https://www.iianalytics.com/analytics-maturity-company-performanceroi.

6   Cam, Arif, Michael Chui, and Bryce Hall. "Survey: AI Adoption Proves Its Worth, but Few Scale Impact." McKinsey. November 22, 2019. https://www.mckinsey.com/featured-insights/artificial-intelligence/global-ai-survey-ai-proves-its-worth-but-few-scale-impact.

7   Ibid.

Chapter 6

How to Get Started with AI?

Now that we understand that organizations can make strategic, tactical, and operational decisions, we turn next to how to get started with AI initiatives. Organizations can do that today; there's no need to wait. There are tremendous business opportunities that can result from AI. If the COVID-19 pandemic has taught us anything, it's that organizations are resilient and can change and adapt faster than was assumed.

Understand Your Endgame

Probably the most important piece of advice in this book is to understand your endgame. As Stephen R. Covey famously wrote in his *The 7 Habits of Highly Effective People*, "Begin with the End in Mind." Traditionally, organizations have had a business strategy and an analytics strategy. However, this is the wrong approach. AI should fuel business strategy. Typically, organizations define OKRs (objectives and key results) annually. These are essentially the company's strategic goals for the year. To achieve them, organizations will create strategic initiatives, which will normally have one or more projects associated with them. And many of these projects will require data, analytics, and automation.

To get started, consider the following areas:[1,2]

Five Key Areas Where AI Can Be Applied

1. To improve decision-making in organizations

2. To better understand customers/markets

3. To deliver more intelligent services and products

4. To improve internal business processes

5. To monetize data

As with any initiative, organizations should not try to boil the ocean. A few quick-win projects and two or three strategic initiatives should be chosen.

Establish a Culture of Analytics

A survey of business leaders found that 92.9% think that culture is the biggest impediment to success, while only 8.1% cite technology as the biggest obstacle.[3] As with any major initiative, we need to look no further than Kotter's 8-Step Model for Leading Change:[4]

1. **Create a Sense of Urgency**: How does AI map and enable your corporate strategy?

2. **Build a Guiding Coalition**: Have you established a cross-functional AI team at the leadership level to implement AI?

3. **Form a Strategic Vision and Initiatives**: Have you mapped your AI initiatives to KPIs?

4. **Enlist a Volunteer Army**: Have you practiced design thinking and put people at the center of the process?

5. **Enable Action by Removing Barriers**: Does your cross-functional AI Tiger Team (see next section) have all the resources needed to implement AI?

6. **Generate Short-Term Wins**: Are your projects scoped sufficiently to be achievable in a relatively short timeframe?

7. **Sustain Acceleration**: Have you created a culture of innovation?

8. **Institute Change**: Are you ensuring adoption of AI initiatives?

Empower an AI Tiger Team

The next step is to create an AI Tiger Team, which is a cross-functional team that should encompass all the roles needed to drive the project forward. The team should consist of a senior business leader, AI practitioners, automation experts, and business users who will be impacted by the project. Figure 6.1 identifies the major stakeholders associated with an AI Tiger Team.

Figure 6.1: AI Tiger Team

The most critical component that many organizations fail to include is the business and domain experts. Failing to engage with these stakeholders is certain to reduce your chances of success.

To summarize, to realize the benefits of analytics in an organization, the following elements are required:

1. Establish strategic business priorities, objectives, and key results (OKRs).

2. Define, map, and prioritize specific projects for each initiative.

3. Establish cross-functional teams to understand how technology can help achieve stated business objectives.

4. Establish project management and change management processes and plans.

5. Understand the data required to make the decision.

6. Understand analytic techniques required to make the decision.

7. Partner with end users, domain experts, and business stakeholders and then iterate on a solution.

8. Track progress, learn from failures, and celebrate success.

Innovation-Oriented Cultures

Innovation-oriented cultures do things differently; they do not place blame and are more optimistic. Assuming you have well-defined strategic initiatives and projects, you can take specific steps to help build an analytic culture. Analytics are different; unlike IT or other corporate projects, not every AI experiment or investigation will bear fruit. In fact, the analytics process is full of successes and failures. The trick is knowing when to walk away. However, when one of your initiatives fails, consider the following steps:[5]

1. Acknowledge the failure.

2. Describe the failure.

3. Describe options for recovery or remediation.

4. Discuss the best path forward.

5. Decide whether to regroup and work toward obtaining the original objective or move to the next challenge.

6. Try again.

This is quite similar to the PDCA (Plan Do Check Act) process that I used when in manufacturing. PDCA is a four-step model for implementing change that is commonly used in lean manufacturing. The ultimate goal of PDCA is to foster a culture of continuous improvement, which is what AI-driven organizations should foster as well.

It is important to continually foster an innovation-oriented culture. Once people start pointing fingers at one another, organizations tend to become stymied and risk adverse. Remember, the steps in the AI project lifecycle are iterative in nature. There are continual trade-offs and multiple paths a project team can take. When you think you're on the cusp of a big breakthrough there can be another set back. Correspondingly, when you're just about to lose all hope and abandon a project, you can have a eureka moment! Continually innovate and maintain a positive attitude to get the results you desire.

Invest in Analytics and Data Literacy

Data literacy can be defined as:

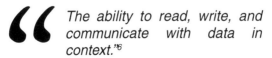

The ability to read, write, and communicate with data in context."[6]

It consists of two components—vocabulary and skills.[7]

For someone to be considered data literate, the person needs to understand the language (or jargon) of data and analytics. Some of this was covered in Chapter 3 and includes:

- Data, analytic, and automation terms and concepts (e.g., ML, NLG, computer vision, RPA, metadata)
- Analysis methods and concepts (e.g., supervised, unsupervised, and reinforcement learning)
- Value drivers, business decisions, and business outcomes (e.g., strategic vs. operational vs. tactical decisions)

And the skills required include the ability to:

- Think critically about projects.
- Collaborate with others across organizational boundaries.
- Be curious.
- Correctly frame business problems so they can be solved with data, analytics, and automation.

Being data literate is foundational to the adoption and usage of AI across an organization.

What Do High-Performing Companies Do Differently?

There are several things high-performing companies do differently:

- Align strategy to business goals.
- Invest in talent and training.
- Collaborate across functions.
- Apply strong data practices.

- Establish standard protocols and repeatable methodologies.
- Ensure adoption and value.

Figure 6.2 illustrates these practices, along with the percentage of respondents saying the given statement is true.

Figure 6.2: High-Performing Practices

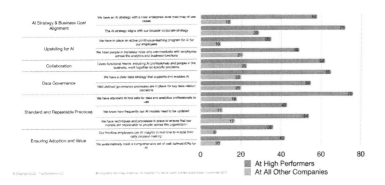

Summary

In this chapter, we examined how to get started with AI. Smart organizations understand their endgame, create a culture of analytics, invest in people, and use a specific set of practices to ensure AI success. Top-performing companies align their AI strategy with business goals, upskill for AI, collaborate across teams, have data governance and standard and repeatable processes, and ensure AI adoption and value.

In Chapter 8, we will provide some practical next steps and a template based on these key practices.

Chapter 6 References

1   Marr, Bernard. The Intelligence Revolution: Transforming Your Business with AI. New York: Kogan Page, 2020.

2   "DATAcated Conference: Bernard Marr; How to Develop a Data Strategy [video]." YouTube. November 1, 2020. https://youtu.be/e7QVnXDGVlw.

3   Davenport, Thomas, and Randy Bean. "Data and AI Leadership Executive Survey 2022." NewVantage Partners. 2022. https://c6abb8db-514c-4f5b-b5a1-fc710f1e464e.filesusr.com/ugd/e5361a_2f859f3457f24cff9b2f8a2bf54f82b7.pdf.

4   Kotter, John. "The 8-Step Process for Leading Change." Kotter. 2020. https://www.kotterinc.com/8-steps-process-for-leading-change/.

5   Thompson, John K. Building Analytics Teams: Harnessing Analytics and Artificial Intelligence for Business Improvement. Birmingham, UK: Packt, 2020.

6   Morrow, Jordan. Be Data Literate the Data Literacy Skills Everyone Needs to Succeed. New York: Kogan Page, 2021.

7   "Webinar: 7 Ways to Build the Case for Data Literacy (and What If You Don't?!) [video]." YouTube. November 10, 2020. https://www.youtube.com/watch?v=eQyhTsOnt2Y&feature=youtu.be.

Chapter 7

Ethical Considerations

Artificial intelligence has the power to transform businesses, ways of working, and consumer habits. A recent survey found that 77% of consumers are very or somewhat likely to trust AI recommendations, while 43% stated they would have a more positive perception of a company if it were more transparent about how AI was used.[9] This begs the question: Are there specific types of recommendations that are more trustworthy? Studies show that if the recommendations are functional or utilitarian in nature (e.g., recommendations for new refrigerators, Netflix shows, or TVs), humans are more likely to trust those compared to those that are experiential or emotional in nature (e.g., recommendations for fine wines or health spas).[10] So, most of us would trust AI to pick out the next movie to watch but we're not quite ready for it to plan our next wedding or dream vacation!

Now that we better understand consumer preferences, organizations need to create AI systems that are fair, trustworthy, and unbiased. There are many examples where AI is producing biased results. Examples include recidivism results in the criminal justice system against minorities, unfair hiring practices against women, and even in language translation services.[11]

So, how can organizations ensure that AI is trustworthy?

Don't Be Creepy

The first tip for businesses: Don't be creepy. Just because you can do something doesn't mean you should. In 2012, the retail giant Target created a pregnancy prediction model.[12] With uncanny accuracy, the company could predict if a female was pregnant based on her purchases. Using data science and ML, it was discovered that women would purchase unscented lotion and specific vitamin supplements during the second trimester. With this knowledge, Target began to send pregnancy-related coupons to women who were likely to be expecting.

Fast forward a year—an upset father stormed into the Minneapolis Target demanding an explanation as to why his daughter was receiving baby coupons. The store manager didn't know why but apologized to the angry father. A few days later, the manager called to apologize again. This time, however, the father was quite embarrassed. He let the store manager know that, unbeknownst to him, his daughter was in fact pregnant.

Even though this was a public relations disaster for Target, it didn't cease sending coupons, it simply became more cunning about it. "Then we started mixing in all these ads for things we knew pregnant women would never buy so the baby ads looked random. We'd put an ad for a lawn mower next to diapers. We'd put a coupon for wineglasses next to infant clothes. That way, it looked like all the products were chosen by chance. And we found out that as long as a pregnant woman thinks she hasn't been spied on, she'll use the coupons. She just assumes that everyone else on her block got the same mailer for diapers and cribs. As long as we don't spook her, it works."[13]

In our digital world, it should be no surprise that companies are constantly monitoring every click, keystroke, and check-in so it can be better understood who you are, what your habits and preferences are, and who you hang out with. For most companies, the goal is to send you a better coupon. I was once discussing salaries of potential data scientists with an individual from the CIA who said, "We have the world's greatest minds working hard to send you a coupon," implying that her organization—although doing very interesting and innovative work—was having trouble competing with the salaries of the private sector. Why was the Target story so outrageous? Was it too direct? Is it any better to mix the specific coupons together in a larger mailer?

I'm not going to analyze the "creepiness factor," but organizations need to understand how data is collected, why it's being collected, and ultimately how it will be used. Companies need to be transparent with users and ask if this information is sensitive or private? Should we even collect that type of information? Who in the organization should have the access to it? What do we intend to do with it? Of course, it's certainly a delicate balance, but don't be creepy—you could put your organization's reputation and future at risk.

Fairness and Bias

When creating AI models, one should go to great lengths to ensure they are fair and unbiased. But this begs the question: What does fair and unbiased mean?

Fairness is the process of understanding bias introduced by your data, algorithms, and automation practices—and ensuring your AI system provides equitable predictions and outcomes across all demographic groups and protected classes.

Where does bias come from? Unfortunately, it can be introduced across many stages of the machine learning (ML) process.

The "**seven sources of harm**" in ML include:[14]

1. Historical bias
2. Representation bias
3. Measurement bias
4. Aggregation bias
5. Learning bias
6. Evaluation bias
7. Deployment bias

Examples include:

- **Algorithmic prejudice and proxies** *(measurement and aggregation bias)*: When features or variables are selected for ML models, the attributes selected could have a significant impact on the biases of a model. Variables such as gender, religious affiliation, age, education level, or years of experience are often recoded to numbers (i.e., male and female becomes a 1 or 0) that make them hard to spot. More interesting is that combining geography and surname or even zip code information is a proxy for race and ethnicity.[15,16]

- **Data collection** (representation bias): When creating AI pipelines, data scientists need to make sure there is equal representation across demographic groups in the training data mimicking those of the overall population. For example, most facial algorithms are extremely biased against 18-to-30-year olds, females, and dark-skinned individuals. In fact, with some of these algorithms "28 members of Congress, disproportionately people of color, were incorrectly matched with mug shot images."[17]

- **Framing the problem**: Let's examine credit risk. How do you define the "creditworthiness" of an individual? Is it the ability to maximize profitability or the number of loans that get repaid? An AI system could maximize profit by simply giving out more subprime loans. But is this in the organizations best interest? This source of bias is interesting because these are business decisions that need to be made and are not necessary ML problems that data scientists alone should be making.

- **Historical bias**: This occurs when the collected data is inherently biased based on the world around us. As an example, when you look at machine translations, words like "nurse" are associated with women and "engineer" with men. This even extends to gender neutral languages like Turkish and Finnish.[18]

- **Underestimation** (representation bias): This occurs when there are not enough representative samples in the data used to train the models. An example is Amazon's AI recruiting system that was biased against women[19] because it was trained using the company's historical data, which was mostly based on men. There are also examples where Black individuals received 30%–50% fewer job callbacks when their resume contained race or ethnicity information.[20]

Now, many data scientists understand how to minimize or reduce these biases when working on an ML project. However, even if everything is considered, the outcome of the AI system could be biased. That's why organizations not only need to have a system in place at the project development level, but also at the outcome level to ensure there are no emergent behaviors or unintended consequences. Why did our **Frogger** only go forward?

Transparent and Explainable

When digital decisions are made in organizations, it must be ensured that the decision is fair, unbiased, and transparent. Businesses need to be prepared to answer questions like:

- Why did you reject my medical insurance claim?
- Why did you reject my job application?

- Why was my credit or loan application rejected?

One of the most important things about digital decisions is that a business cannot say a decision was made because the "algorithm told us to do so." No matter if you're a government agency, corporation, educational institution, or small businesses, it is YOUR obligation to ensure that digital decisions are fair and unbiased—YOUR responsibility to ensure that the decisions are explainable and transparent. In fact, there are many regulations that specifically require and mandate a "right to explanation" for algorithmic decisions.

Data Ethics

Data ethics deals with the practices and procedures used to collect, store, protect, and use an individual's personally identifiable information (PII). This includes data like social security numbers (SSNs), full name, address, phone number, date of birth, drivers license, medical information, biometric data, etc. The fundamental questions that organizations need to ask are "Can we use the data in this way?" and "Should we use the data this way?" Protecting your customers' data is essential. In the United States, there is a Federal Data Strategy that spans the collection, processing, dissemination, use, storage, and disposition of data. Core principles of data ethics include:

- **Ownership** is a concept that individuals have the right to possess their personal information. If you look at apps, many have a clause that states the company has a royalty-free right to use your information in perpetuity. With data ethics, we're bringing the ownership back to the individual. For a business, you always need to ask for permission to use data.

- **Transparency** means that individuals have a right to know how their information is going to be used. You see this with cookies on websites. There is usually some pop-up that says,

"We may track your behavior to personalize the experience." However, many of us are not aware that we are tracked across all our web browsing, not just that site!

- **Privacy and confidentiality** means that if you collect PII data—which may include name, date of birth, mailing address, social security number, bank account info, health info, phone number, and many more—that you will do everything in your power to make sure its stored securely and used sparingly. How much is privacy worth? Facebook stated that Apple's privacy push would cost it $10B in 2022.[21]

- **Honesty, integrity, and intention** means that you should not collect any and all data just because it could be interesting and useful at some point in the future. Organizations should understand why data is collected, how it will be used, and only collect that specific data and nothing more.

- **Accountability** means that all stakeholders using the data are using it appropriately. There needs to be a governance system in place. Companies need to be aware of the usage, privacy, and limitations associated with the data collected and should only use it for the purpose for which it was collected.

GDPR

The European Union (EU) passed the General Data Protection Regulation (GDPR), a framework to protect personal data. There is much to be discussed about GDPR but it would be another TinyTechGuide in itself. Let's focus on Article 6, which defines general principles and the rights of people, otherwise known as data subjects, within the framework.

In order to process an individual's (aka data subject's) data, the following conditions need to be upheld by the entity collecting it:

- Individuals have to give consent to the processing of their data.

- Processing can occur to fulfill contractual obligations with the person.

So, essentially, this is saying that you need to give consent to have your data processed. Are there other situations where your data can be processed without consent? But of course there are! These are the main legal requirements of the entity processing an individual's data:

- To comply with a legal obligation of the data controller or processor.

- To process the data to protect the interests of another data subject.

- To process an individuals data to comply with official authorities or in the public interest

- When the rights of the data subject are overridden, especially in the case of children.

For the person or data subject, the following are key elements of GDPR:

- The data processor must ensure that an individual **giving consent** is provided information in clear, plain language.

- People have the **right to access personal information** and understand how it is being processed.

- Individuals can **transfer their personal data from one entity to another**, known as data portability.

- The **right to be forgotten**, meaning an individual has the right to have personal information removed from Internet searches and other directories.

- The **right to not have information used for automated decisions** and marketing purposes.

As you can see, this is only a small subset of what organizations need to consider when doing business in the European Union (EU). This is something that organizations need to take seriously by thoroughly understanding the regulations.

Ethical Frameworks

As AI continues to evolve, there are more than 80 different ethical guidelines and frameworks in existence.[22] A few of the best include:

- **Ethics guidelines for trustworthy artificial intelligence**: The European Commission defined seven principles for trustworthy AI (covered in more detail later in this chapter). The commission stated that for AI to be trustworthy, it needed to be lawful, ethical, and robust.

- **OECD AI Principles**: The Organization for Economic Co-operation and Development is an international organization with 38 member countries. Its goal is to improve lives though better policies. The OECD principles include:[23]

  - Inclusive growth, sustainable development, and well-being
  - Human-centered values and fairness
  - Transparency and explainability
  - Robustness, security, and safety
  - Accountability

- **Partnership on AI**: Its mission is to bring "diverse voices together across global sectors, disciplines, and demographics so developments in AI advanced positive outcomes for people and society."[24]

- **AI Ethics from IBM**: Pillars include notions of explainability, fairness, transparency, and privacy.[25]

- **Responsible AI practices from Google**: Google's guidelines include using a human-centered design approach, identifying metrics for training and monitoring, examining raw data, testing, understanding the limitations of data and modeling, and deployment monitoring and updates.[26]

- **Responsible AI practices from Microsoft**: Microsoft's responsible AI practices include topics such as fairness, reliability and safety, privacy and security, inclusiveness, transparency, and accountability.[27]

There are six principles common across most frameworks:

1. Human-centered with respect for human rights
2. Fair, equitable, and just
3. Do no harm
4. Transparency and explainability
5. Responsibility and accountability
6. Privacy and security

The EU Ethical Guidelines for Trustworthy AI

In April 2019, the European Commission's independent High-Level Expert Group on Artificial Intelligence published a report entitled "Ethics Guidelines for Trustworthy AI."

Foundational Principles for Trustworthy AI

The report defined three guiding principles for building trustworthy AI:[28]

1. **Lawful**: The AI system should be respectful of the law and local regulations.

2. **Ethical**: The AI system should be ethical and adhere to ethical principles and values.

3. **Robust**: Since AI could do significant harm, it should be robust from a technical and social perspective.

Now, one may wonder how to apply this across political boundaries. What is lawful and ethical in one region of the world may not be in another.

For example, some countries use apps to monitor, track, and censor citizens. Some of the systems are designed to suppress certain minority groups, while others use a public-shaming approach. Names and faces may be displayed on public billboards for things the state deems unacceptable—like jaywalking or your dog doing his business in someone else's yard.

Now, my goal is not to impose my morals or pass judgment, but a multinational company has many things to consider when operating across geopolitical boundaries. A "one-size-fits-all" approach may not be appropriate or acceptable.

Figure 7.1 outlines the EU Union's AI ethics framework.

Figure 7.1: European Union's AI Ethics Framework

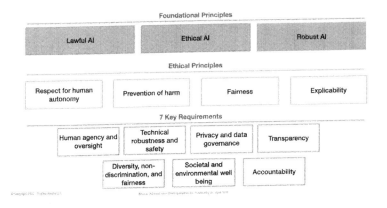

Four ethical principles result from the three foundational principles (lawful, ethical, and robust). The EU believes that there are a set of "indivisible rights" set forth in international human rights law and that AI-system designers should aspire to support "ethical imperatives" contextualized for AI systems:[29]

- **Respect for human autonomy**: This principle states that humans should be self-sufficient and have freedom. Essentially, people should remain in control and enabled to take part in the democratic process. AI should not try to deceive, manipulate, coerce, subordinate, deceive, or herd humans.

- **Prevention of harm**: Quite simply, AI systems should not cause physical, mental, or emotional harm. Since AI can affect a wide population very quickly because of asymmetries of information or power, AI designers should make sure that the output is monitored to ensure that citizens, employers, businesses, consumers, and governments are not being manipulated.

- **Fairness**: AI systems should not be biased or discriminatory and should strive to have an equal and unbiased distribution of "benefits and costs." In essence, people's choices should not be undermined. Everyone has a choice! "Fairness implies that AI practitioners should respect the principle of proportionality between means and ends, and consider carefully how to balance competing interests and objectives."[30]

- **Explicability**: AI systems need to be transparent and interpretable. Everyone has a right to an explanation. Why were you denied your car loan? Or that job? Everyone has the right to know why specific decisions have been made. They have a right to an explanation as to why the AI made a certain decision. This includes an understanding of the factors that led to the decision. For the organization utilizing AI, it needs to be able to provide traceability, auditability, reproducibility, and transparency as to why a specific decision regarding a specific individual was made.

In the 2002 movie *Minority Report*, if a "recog" predicts that a future crime will be committed, you would be arrested. As AI becomes more embedded in society, these sorts of questions are sure to become more prominent. At some level, it becomes philosophical—does one have free will or is fate pre-determined? If you have a high probability to re-offend but have served your sentence, should you remain in jail?

The EU framework discusses the inherent conflict between different principles. Does individual liberty and freedom trump societal benefits? Is predictive policing fair and unbiased? If the algorithm "decides" that a person is likely to commit a crime or re-offend, should society take preventative action?

Key Requirements for Trustworthy AI

Based on the guidelines, the EU framework then outlines the following seven requirements:

- **Human agency and oversight**: No AI system should operate completely autonomously and should respect fundamental human rights. AI should augment human decisions and not replace them. There needs to be a process for challenging decisions by those impacted by an AI system. This means having a human in the loop (HITL) that can override a decision if appropriate.

- **Technical robustness and safety:** AI systems need to be secure, robust, and not vulnerable to cyber attacks. Predictions must be accurate, and systems should be reliable (i.e., accept a wide variety of inputs) and reproducible. Organizations need to take cybersecurity seriously. If there is an attack, there needs to be a fallback plan. In addition to normal security requirements, attacks on AI systems can use different methods and strategies. Take "adversarial data poisoning."[31] This is an attack where a bad actor tries to alter the data used to train models that would cause it to make bad predictions with new input data. As an example, your self-driving car could misclassify stop and speed limit signs.[32]

- **Privacy and governance**: AI systems need to respect an individual's privacy and ensure that the data being used is of the utmost quality. Related to the second principle (technical robustness and safety), AI designers need to ensure that malicious data is not fed into the system (i.e., data poisoning). Only authorized users should be able to access an individual's data and it must be ensured that data is fair, unbiased, and adheres to all privacy regulations throughout its entire lifecycle.

- **Transparency**: Organizations need to be able to trace the lineage of data and understand its source, how it was collected, how it was transformed, and ultimately, how it is used. This needs to be auditable and model outputs should be explainable (see the Apple credit card example). Also, people who are interacting with AI should be aware that they are interacting with it.

- **Diversity, nondiscrimination, and fairness**: AI needs to treat all groups equally. To achieve this, designers need to include people from diverse cultures, experiences, and backgrounds. AI should be accessible to everyone, regardless of any disabilities or other factors.

- **Societal and environmental well-being**: AI designers should strive to improve society, encourage democracy, and make systems as environmentally friendly and sustainable as possible. As we have seen with Facebook and the 2020 US election, AI can negatively (or positively) impact society, so the leaders of organizations need to think about this critically.

- **Accountability**: AI system designers should be accountable for the systems they design, which need to be auditable and incorporate a way for those impacted by decisions to rectify and correct any unfair decisions. Furthermore, designers may be held liable for any harm done to individuals or groups.

Although these principles make intuitive sense, there is "substantive divergence in relation to how these principles are interpreted, why they are deemed important, what issue, domain or actors they pertain to, and how they should be implemented."[33]

Additional AI Ethical Frameworks

In the United States, the "Executive Order on Promoting the Use of Trustworthy Artificial Intelligence in the Federal Government" outlines the following nine principles for the use of AI:[34]

Lawful and respectful of our Nation's values

1. Purposeful and performance-driven

2. Accurate, reliable, and effective

3. Safe, secure, and resilient

4. Understandable

5. Responsible and traceable

6. Regularly monitored

7. Transparent

8. Accountable

Summary

In this chapter, we discussed the common principles across data and AI-ethics frameworks. At its foundation, data ethics and the GDPR regulations are a good starting point. There may be situations where there is friction and tension between the various principles and human goals, which can be difficult to express with a mathematical formula. Companies need to think critically about AI output and make sure their systems are fair, unbiased, and transparent.

Chapter 7 References

1   "Report: 43% of Consumers Feel Transparency Is Key for Positive AI Innovations." VentureBeat. January 4, 2022. https://venturebeat.com/2022/01/04/report-43-of-consumers-feel-transparency-is-key-for-positive-ai-innovations/.

2   Longoni, Chiara, and Luca Cian. "When Do We Trust AI's Recommendations More than People's?" Harvard Business Review. October 14, 2020. https://hbr.org/2020/10/when-do-we-trust-ais-recommendations-more-than-peoples.

3   Mcgregor, Sean. "When AI Systems Fail: Introducing the AI Incident Database." Partnership on AI. November 18, 2020. https://www.partnershiponai.org/aiincidentdatabase/.

4   Duhigg, Charles. "How Companies Learn Your Secrets." New York Times. February 16, 2012. https://www.nytimes.com/2012/02/19/magazine/shopping-habits.html.

5   Ibid.

6   Suresh, Harini, and John Guttag. "A Framework for Understanding Unintended Consequences of Machine Learning." arXiv. 2021. https://arxiv.org/pdf/1901.10002.pdf.

7   Datta, Anupam. "3 Kinds of Bias in AI Models: And How We Can Address Them." InfoWorld. February 24, 2021. https://www.infoworld.com/article/3607748/3-kinds-of-bias-in-ai-models-and-how-we-can-address-them.html.

8 "Using Publicly Available Information to Proxy for Unidentified Race and Ethnicity." Consumer Financial Protection Bureau. 2014. https://www.consumerfinance.gov/data-research/research-reports/using-publicly-available-information-to-proxy-for-unidentified-race-and-ethnicity/.

9 Najibi, Alex. "Racial Discrimination in Face Recognition Technology." Science in the News. October 24, 2020. https://sitn.hms.harvard.edu/flash/2020/racial-discrimination-in-face-recognition-technology/.

10 Savoldi, Beatrice, Marco Gaido, Luisa Bentivogli, Matteo Negri, and Marco Turchi. "Gender Bias in Machine Translation." Transactions of the Association for Computational Linguistics 9 (2021): 845–74. https://doi.org/10.1162/tacl_a_00401.

11 Dastin, Jeffrey. "Amazon Scraps Secret AI Recruiting Tool That Showed Bias against Women." Reuters. October 10, 2018. https://www.reuters.com/article/us-amazon-com-jobs-automation-insight/amazon-scraps-secret-ai-recruiting-tool-that-showed-bias-against-women-idUSKCN1MK08G.

12 Zapata, Dawn. "New Study Finds AI-Enabled Anti-Black Bias in Recruiting." Thomson Reuters Institute. June 18, 2021. https://www.thomsonreuters.com/en-us/posts/legal/ai-enabled-anti-black-bias/.

13 Owusu, Tony. "Facebook Says Apple's Privacy Push Will Cost $10B (But Can't Stop It)." TheStreet. February 3, 2022. https://www.thestreet.com/investing/facebook-says-apples-privacy-push-will-cost-10b-but-cant-stop-it.

14 Rakova, Bogdana, Jingying Yang, Henriette Cramer, and Rumman Chowdhury. "Where Responsible AI Meets Reality." Proceedings of the ACM on Human-Computer Interaction 5, no. CSCW1 (2021): 1–23. https://doi.org/10.1145/3449081.

15 "The OECD Artificial Intelligence (AI) Principles." OECD. n.d. Accessed March 17, 2022. https://oecd.ai/en/ai-principles.

16 "Home." Partnership on AI. n.d. Accessed January 16, 2022. https://partnershiponai.org/about/.

17 "AI Ethics." IBM. n.d. Accessed March 17, 2022. https://www.ibm.com/artificial-intelligence/ethics.

18 "Responsible AI Practices." Google AI. 2019. https://ai.google/responsibilities/responsible-ai-practices/.

19 "Responsible AI Principles from Microsoft." Microsoft. n.d. Accessed March 17, 2022. https://www.microsoft.com/en-us/ai/responsible-ai.

20 "Ethics Guidelines for Trustworthy AI: Shaping Europe's Digital Future." European Commission. March 8, 2021. https://digital-strategy.ec.europa.eu/en/library/ethics-guidelines-trustworthy-ai.

21 Ibid.

22 Ibid.

23 Poremba, Sue. "Data Poisoning: When Attackers Turn AI and ML against You." Security Intelligence. April 21, 2021. https://securityintelligence.com/articles/data-poisoning-ai-and-machine-learning/.

24 Wang, Chen, Jian Chen, Yang Yang, Xiaoqiang Ma, and Jiangchuan Liu. "Poisoning Attacks and Countermeasures in Intelligent Networks: Status Quo and Prospects." Digital Communications and Networks (July 2021). https://doi.org/10.1016/j.dcan.2021.07.009.

25 Jobin, Anna, Marcello Ienca, and Effy Vayena. "The Global Landscape of AI Ethics Guidelines." Nature Machine Intelligence 1, no. 9 (2019): 389–99. https://doi.org/10.1038/s42256-019-0088-2.

26 Executive Office of the President. "Executive Order 13960: Promoting the Use of Trustworthy Artificial Intelligence in the Federal Government." Federal Register. 2020. https://www.federalregister.gov/documents/2020/12/08/2020-27065/promoting-the-use-of-trustworthy-artificial-intelligence-in-the-federal-government.

Chapter 8

The Road Ahead

Both data and AI ethics are paramount to any transformation initiative. Without them, you may end up in the headlines of a major publication or the chyron of a TV show, creating a PR nightmare beyond your wildest dreams. In this final chapter, I discuss the road ahead and some questions and best practices to consider along your AI journey. At the end, I provide a template with critical questions to ask that will help accelerate your AI journey. This template is based on the A3 template of my lean manufacturing days. For those not familiar with an A3 template, it does refer to the paper size and essentially represents a plan on a page for improving projects.

Be SMART and Determine Your Strategic Direction

In order to scale AI, organizations need to think carefully about their strategy. The trick is to not boil the ocean but rather to pick a few high-value projects that will improve the customer experience or the bottom line.

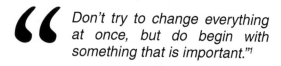

Don't try to change everything at once, but do begin with something that is important."[1]

An organization needs to think holistically about the process it wishes to reimagine. In selecting the process, keep the SMART goals in mind. That is, the project should be specific, measurable, actionable, realistic, and have a timeline.

Business leaders should avoid a big-bang, waterfall-type mentality. There are two keys to AI success:

1. The project selected should be meaningful. Organizations should follow agile practices and show demonstrable progress over the course of a year. The shorter the agile cycle, the higher the likelihood of success.[2]

2. The project should not require the organization to re-architect its entire data and analysis infrastructure. Sure, you may need some new tools, but the organization should be able to achieve value with its existing infrastructure.

Later, I'll provide a template to help frame your thoughts around this, but first, consider the following questions for your organization:

1. Understand your endgame: Identify your strategic business imperatives.

2. Identify how this will create business value in any of the following:

   - Top-line growth
   - Bottom-line returns
   - Efficiency gains
   - Improved customer satisfaction
   - Reduced cost
   - Reduced risk

Reimagine Your Business Processes

In the end, there are two approaches an organization can take. The first is where most start. It automates, optimizes, digitizes, and improves existing processes, or reimagines existing processes. There is surely significant value in optimizing existing processes, but this will not be enough to achieve a sustainable competitive advantage.

To achieve that, companies need to take the latter approach: reimagining their existing ways of doing business. **AI is not magic, and digitizing outmoded and legacy processes will simply bake inefficiencies into your business.** Organizations need to rethink how work gets done and how AI can help change the very nature of how it gets done.

Consider the following questions regarding your business:

1. What is your reimagined business process? How is the new process different?

2. Have you identified and mapped KPIs to the business process?

3. Which use cases contribute to the business process?

4. How can AI help achieve your goals?

5. What data is required for this business process?

Create a Culture of Analytics and Upskill Employees

When COVID-19 disrupted the very fabric of how people work, employers scrambled to retrain employees to learn new technologies and ways of working. However, to achieve a sustainable competitive advantage, companies need to empower employees, increase AI literacy, and create a culture of analytics across the business. Many organizations are now looking to upskill their workforce.

Upskilling is a strategic investment made by organizations. The goal is improving the knowledge, skills, and proficiencies that help employees advance their careers.

There are three key steps to create a successful upskilling program across an organization:

1. **Determine the organization's priorities and skill gaps**. Before businesses can create an upskilling plan, leaders need to understand which skills are required today and which will be in the future.

2. **Give employees the power to take charge of their careers**. As organizational priorities change and new technology is introduced, organizations need to retrain employees. Those that can adapt to new roles have a more rewarding experience. The manager plays a critical role in understanding how employees would like to grow their career. Although managers need to provide career and training opportunities to help employees' progress, the employees themselves need to take charge.

3. **Sense, respond, and listen**. If the Great Resignation has taught us anything, it's that if employees are dissatisfied they'll simply quit and find a new job. Through employee surveys, exit surveys, and other means, managers need to listen carefully to their workforce. If employees are sending consistent messages in the surveys, management needs to act quickly to remediate the situation.

4. **Provide a guide**. Many employees may not be fully aware of the opportunities that exist in their organization. Learning and development teams need to provide guidance to employees on the steps to upskill and become more mobile within the company.

5. **Provide the time.** This step is often overlooked. Organizations need to make sure that employees have the time and training materials needed to begin the upskilling journey.

6. **Measure results and impact**. If you can measure it, you can improve it. Organizations need to make sure the right systems are in place to measure reskilling and upskilling initiatives, as well as the impact these initiatives have on the bottom line.

Regarding your organization, consider these questions:

1. Who is involved in the business processes?

2. How will work change as a result?

3. Who is in the AI Tiger Team that can bring the project to fruition?

4. Is there a project and change management plan in place?

5. Are there training programs in place?

6. Does a center of excellence (CoE) need to be established?

Creating a culture of analytics starts with leadership. Business leaders need to continually communicate and reinforce that AI is critical to the organization's success.

Understand and Mitigate the Risks

As mentioned, there are a variety of risks and ethical elements to consider in an AI system. We live in an ever-changing, dynamic world—data is constantly changing. We need to make sure that AI systems are constantly monitored to avoid any unintended consequences. Since AI has the power to affect large numbers of people, we need to monitor both the practices used to create AI systems as well as the output of the decision framework.

For initiatives, consider:

1. What are the regulatory risks?

2. What are the reputational risks?

3. Do I have the skills to do this alone?

4. Who owns the risk mitigation strategy?

5. How can ethical AI practice be implemented?

Design Thinking

Many elements for success center on design thinking, which is a human-centric approach to rapid problem-solving. This is important because humans are at the center of the AI revolution. The key elements behind design thinking include:

- **Wicked problems** describe difficulties that refuse to be solved using standard methods and approaches. These are problems that are difficult to define, and attempts to solve them usually lead to uncovering more problems.

- **Rapid iteration and experimentation.** Since design thinking is tackling "wicked problems," it's important to have quick iterations of ideas by continually trying new methods and activities.

- **Human centered** is a tenant that aims to put people at the center of the solution ideation. It is your employees who are the source for inspiration and innovation, not the technology. Many describe this as empathy.

- **Produce something rather than nothing**. Don't wait for AI solutions to manifest themselves. Many organizations fall into the trap of "what-if" and assume an ultimate be-all and end-all solution. My advice: Don't sit around and brainstorm about potential solutions. Yes, planning is important, but we need to get things done. A core principle for design thinking is a bias towards action. Remember PDCA? Rather than waiting for the perfect solution, create an innovation culture where people want to continually improve.

If your organization keeps people at the center of the process, it'll be much better off.

Using AI for Good

Lastly, although AI has the power to potentially disrupt societies, I'm a firm believe that it will be used as a force multiplier for social good. It has the power to create tremendous opportunities for people and improve their well-being. The AI for Good program is an ongoing effort designed to address the United Nation's Sustainable Development Goals (SDGs). These 17 interlinked goals have 169 KPIs used to track progress toward the 2030 Agenda for Sustainable Development. The goals generally align to five key themes: people, planet, prosperity, peace, and partnership.

- **People**: AI has great potential to help people escape poverty. Although those in extreme poverty have declined from 16% in 2010 to 10% in 2015, there is still much work to be done.[3] AI is being used to develop highly-detailed poverty maps that help get the right resources to the right people.[4] It is also being used in precision agriculture to allow farmers to do more with less, as well as improve crop yields, detect diseases, and provide the best techniques for pest mitigation strategies.

- **Planet**: AI is being heavily depended upon to reduce the effects of climate change. It is used for automated environmental monitoring (e.g., algae blooms, wildfires, etc.) and to better predict weather. AI plays a critical role in everything from better understanding where to put renewable energy plants to cutting greenhouse gas emissions to precision agriculture. It is projected to help cut greenhouse gas emissions 4% by 2030.[5]

- **Peace:** There are of course AI initiatives to build better weapons, but I choose to focus on the positive. AI can be used to help achieve world peace. Although it has been attributed to creating and exacerbating division on social media, I hold out hope that it will also bring people together. AI is used to deliver better police services, including surveillance and monitoring. One study stated that smart technologies such as AI could help cities reduce crime by 30% to 40% and reduce response times for emergency services by 20% to 35%.[6]

The other two themes, prosperity and partnership, are critical to the SDGs. Governments cannot do it on their own—they need all of our organizations to contribute. If we can put people at the center of the AI experience, eliminating poverty, hunger, sickness, scarcity will follow and prosperity and peace strengthened.

There are several data sets available for use related to the above topics at https://ai4good.org/ai-for-sdgs/.

A Bright Future

For many organizations, the road ahead is uncharted. There will be successes, failures, setbacks, and breakthroughs. It's all part of the AI journey to clearly communicate your strategy, be agile, and transform your organization with a culture of analytics. Many of the elements described above speak directly to the application of design thinking and the ideation and delivery of AI in most organizations. Design thinking puts the human at the center of solutions.

With everything I've shared in this book, I hope you realize that AI is not *The Terminator*; it's more approachable than you think. AI is simply a fusion of data + analytics + automation. It is being used across every industry and line of business. So, we're not at the point where AI is a sentient being; rather, it's something here to help us. AI provides the ability to order a pizza of the upmost quality (inspected by AI) and have our house mapped and cleaned by a Roomba® (autonomous robotic vacuum cleaner).

AI has the power to entirely transform organizations and societies. Every department and industry can use AI to gain a competitive advantage. Organizations need to take data and AI ethics seriously or risk losing the confidence of the public. In the end, AI is more approachable and pedestrian than you may think—and it's your people who have the power to unleash it in your organization.

And so, our AI discussion has come to an end. I hope you now have a better understanding of how to apply artificial intelligence in your organization. As you embark on your journey, please share your success, failures, and best practices with me so I can pass the knowledge along to others.

Chapter 8 References

1   Fountaine, Tim, Brian McCarthy, and Tamim Saleh. "Getting AI to Scale." Harvard Business Review. May 1, 2021. https://hbr.org/2021/05/getting-ai-to-scale.

2   Bughin, Jacques, Tanguy Catlin, and Laura LaBerge. "Digital Leaders Accelerate Their Pace and Magnitude." McKinsey. June 2019. https://www.mckinsey.com/business-functions/mckinsey-digital/our-insights/the-drumbeat-of-digital-how-winning-teams-play.

3   Mhlanga, David. "Artificial Intelligence in the Industry 4.0, and Its Impact on Poverty, Innovation, Infrastructure Development, and the Sustainable Development Goals: Lessons from Emerging Economies?" Sustainability 13, no. 11 (2021): 5788. https://doi.org/10.3390/su13115788.

4   McGorman, Laura, Guanghua Chi, and Han Fang. "How AI-Powered Poverty Maps Can Increase Equity in the COVID-19 Response." Brookings. May 7, 2021. https://www.brookings.edu/blog/future-development/2021/05/07/how-ai-

powered-poverty-maps-can-increase-equity-in-the-covid-19-response/.

5   Nelson, Arthur. "Here's How AI Can Help Fight Climate Change." World Economic Forum. August 11, 2021. https://www.weforum.org/agenda/2021/08/how-ai-can-fight-climate-change/.

6   "Surveillance and Predictive Policing through AI." Deloitte. n.d. Accessed February 26, 2022. https://www2.deloitte.com/global/en/pages/public-sector/articles/urban-future-with-a-purpose/surveillance-and-predictive-policing-through-ai.html.

Template

1. Background: What are you talking about and why?	Your Answer
What is your company's vision? <ul><li>What is the purpose?</li><li>How will AI help achieve the vision?</li><li>What is the business value?</li><li>In what departments will it be applied?</li><li>What business goals need to be improved?</li><li>Top line growth? Bottom line gains?</li><li>Reduced costs?</li><li>Reduced risks?</li><li>Improved productivity?</li><li>Service availability?</li></ul>	

- Improved customer intimacy?

- Organizational upskilling?

What are the strategic, operational, historical or organizational contexts of the situation?

2. Current Conditions: Where do things stand now?	Your Answer
<ul><li>What is the current problem or need? What is the gap in company performance?</li><li>What is happening now versus what you want or need to be happening?</li><li>What KPIs or data indicate there is a problem?</li><li>What specific conditions indicate that you have a problem or need?<ul><li>Where and how much?</li></ul></li><li>Can you break the problem into smaller pieces?<ul><li>Show facts and processes visually using charts, graphs, maps, etc.</li></ul></li></ul>	

3. Future Goal: What specific outcome is required?	Your Answer

What specific goals and success metrics do you need to achieve?

- Goal: Improve customer satisfaction | Metric: NPS Score | Target Value: xxxxx | Date Done: XX

- Goal: Reduce Cost | Metric: Cap Ex/Op Ex | Target value: xxxx| Date Done: XX

- Goal: Reduce Risk | Metric: Fraud Rate | Target Value: xxxx | Date Done: XX

- Goal: Improve service uptime | Metric: % monthly availability | Target Value: xx | Date Done: XX

What projects is the best fit with AI?

- Create map of: Project Name | Alignment to Mission | Sponsor | KPIs Impacted | Business Feasibility | Technical Feasibility

147

Communicate Plan - Show visually how much, by when, and with what impact. • Vision [Goals, Benefits, KPIs] | Impact on Org [Business, process, people] • Risks [Regulations, Ethics, Skills] | Adoption [Use Cases (value maps), Decisions, Governance]	
4. Root Cause Analysis: Why does the problem or need exist?	**Your Answer**
• What do the specifics of the issues in work processes (location, patterns, trends, factors) indicate about why the performance gap or need exists? • What conditions or occurrences are preventing you from achieving the goals? • Why do they exist? What is (are) their cause(s)?	

5. Countermeasures: What do you propose and why?	Your Answer
• What options exist for addressing the gaps and improving performance in the current situation?	
• What are the regulatory, reputational (ethics) or internal risks (i.e. technical debt, talent, resistance to change?)	
• For the top two or three alternatives, how do they compare to one another? Have you factored in effectiveness, feasibility, and potential disruption?	
• What are their relative costs and benefits?	
• Which do you recommend and why?	
• Show how your proposed actions will address the specific causes of the gaps or constraints you identified in your analysis. The link should be specific and map to the issues!	

6. Implementation Plan: How will you implement this?	Your Answer

- What are the main actions and outcomes in the AI implementation process and in what sequence?

- Have you mapped the strategic concerns to solutions, responsible owners, and organizations that will complete the goals?

- Who will be responsible for what, when, and how much? How will you measure effectiveness? When will progress be reviewed and by whom?

- What support and resources will be required?

- Will you form a Tiger Team and CoE? If so, who are the members and roles?

- Map roles to responsibilities to owning departments or individuals

- How will AI impact the organization?

  - Create strategic questions and answers—make this available to the organization.

7. Follow-up Actions: How will you ensure ongoing improvement?	Your Answer
• How and when will you know if the plans outlined have succeeded? Were the plans followed? Did they have the requisite impact?	
• How will you monitor the KPIs?	
• How will you know if you met your objective or reduced the gap in performance?	
• What related issues or unintended consequences do you anticipate?	
• What contingencies can you anticipate? What processes will you use to enable, assure, and sustain success?	
• How will you highlight successes and share your learning with other areas?	

Acknowledgments

Those who have tried writing a book know it's no small endeavor. I would like to acknowledge my family, friends, and colleagues for their support and encouragement.

To my wife, Erin Sweenor, thank you for your feedback on all aspects of the book and TinyTechMedia LLC. Everything you've done has helped shape this book, from cover design to proofreading, general business questions, and pricing. Thanks to you, we now have a published book.

Mom and Dad, thank you for your readthrough and feedback of the initial manuscript. It helped me simplify some of the language in the book.

To Nick Jewell, John Thompson, and Kjell Carlsson, thank you for your early reviews and feedback. Although we don't always agree, your insights have made this book stronger. I also greatly appreciate your endorsements.

Josipa Ćaran Šafradin, thank you for your help on the wonderful cover design and the multiple iterations we went through to get it just right. We now have a system that all other TinyTechGuides will follow.

Taylor Porter, thank you for agreeing to be my editor for the inaugural TinyTechGuide. You have made this book stronger and more consistent.

Ken Sanford, thank you for answering my random questions on economic theory and inflation.

Stephen Archut, I appreciate the conversations we had on modern data management.

Lastly, thanks to Kate Strachnyi, Judith Hurwitz, Ravit Jain, Tom Davenport, Howard Dresner, and Al Herron for agreeing to write endorsements for this book.

Remember, It's not the tech that's tiny, just the book!™

Ever onward!

About the Author

David Sweenor is a thought leader in analytics, an international speaker, author, and co-developer of several patents. David has over 20 years of hands-on business analytics experience, spanning product marketing, strategy, product development, and data warehousing. He specializes in artificial intelligence, machine learning, data science, business intelligence, the Internet of Things (IoT), and manufacturing analytics.

Follow David on Twitter @DavidSweenor and connect with him on LinkedIn https://www.linkedin.com/in/davidsweenor/

Index

Index

public safety 78

R

recruitment 73
recurrent neural networks (RNNs) 72
regression 40
reinforcement learning 41, 48, 60, 116
Renault 67, 68
return on investment (ROI) 107
revenue 4, 10, 11, 34, 77, 81, 82, 84, 107
robotic process automation (RPA) 7, 53, 54, 60, 65, 88, 116
robotics 9, 55, 71
Roomba® 147
root cause analysis 72
routing 65

S

safety 76, 88, 127, 128, 131, 132
sales and parts forecasting 69
Salesforce 56, 64
Samsung 85
  Smart TV 8, 30
scheduling 7, 40, 87
score 24, 107
Securities and Exchange Commission (SEC) 72
self-driving cars 1, 49
semiconductors 68
semi-supervised learning 41
sentiment analysis 73, 74
service ticket categorization 74

Siemens 68
Slack 30
SMART goals 140
smartphone 25, 34, 36, 38, 78
smart sampling 82
social security numbers (SSNs) 124
Sony 28
Starbucks
  Deep Brew AI 67
Stitch Fix 84, 85
stock-keeping unit (SKU) 68
stockout 5, 28
strategic decisions 100, 101
supervised learning 41
supplier risk monitoring 69
supply chain 59, 69
  automation 74
  disruptions 23
  visibility 67, 69, 87

T

tactical decisions 101, 116
talent management 73
Target 120, 121
team
  AI 49
  AI Tiger Team 113, 143
  cross-functional 113
  cross-team collaboration 60
  executive leadership 100
  IT 36, 38, 39, 56, 60
  project 115
  security 60
  software quality 60
text-to-speech technology 50, 51
Tractable 78

Index

Printed in Great Britain
by Amazon

31166571R00099